"After utilizin able to identify threats within my organization to which I was completely unaware. Using my team's knowledge as a competitive advantage, we now have superior systems that save time and energy."

"As a new Chief Technology Officer, I was feeling unprepared and inadequate to be successful in my role. I ordered an IT toolkit Sunday night and was prepared Monday morning to shed light on areas of improvement within my organization. I no longer felt overwhelmed and intimidated, I was excited to share what I had learned."

"I used the questionnaires to interview members of my team. I never knew how many insights we could produce collectively with our internal knowledge."

"I usually work until at least 8pm on weeknights. The Art of Service questionnaire saved me so much time and worry that Thursday night I attended my son's soccer game without sacrificing my professional obligations."

"After purchasing The Art of Service toolkit, I was able to identify areas where my company was not in compliance that could have put my job at risk. I looked like a hero when I proactively educated my team on the risks and presented a solid solution."

"I spent months shopping for an external consultant before realizing that The Art of Service would allow my team to consult themselves! Not only did we save time not catching a consultant up to speed, we were able to keep our company information and industry secrets confidential."

"Everyday there are new regulations and processes in my industry. The Art of Service toolkit has kept me ahead by using AI technology to constantly update the toolkits and address emerging needs."

"I customized The Art of Service toolkit to focus specifically on the concerns of my role and industry. I didn't have to waste time with a generic self-help book that wasn't tailored to my exact situation."

"Many of our competitors have asked us about our secret sauce. When I tell them it's the knowledge we have in-house, they never believe me. Little do they know The Art of Service toolkits are working behind the scenes."

"One of my friends hired a consultant who used the knowledge gained working with his company to advise their competitor. Talk about a competitive disadvantage! The Art of Service allowed us to keep our knowledge from walking out the door along with a huge portion of our budget in consulting fees."

"Honestly, I didn't know what I didn't know. Before purchasing The Art of Service, I didn't realize how many areas of my business needed to be refreshed and improved. I am so relieved The Art of Service was there to highlight our blind spots."

"Before The Art of Service, I waited eagerly for consulting company reports to come out each month. These reports kept us up to speed but provided little value because they put our competitors on the same playing field. With The Art of Service, we have uncovered unique insights to drive our business forward."

"Instead of investing extensive resources into an external consultant, we can spend more of our budget towards pursuing our company goals and objectives...while also spending a little more on corporate holiday parties."

"The risk of our competitors getting ahead has been mitigated because The Art of Service has provided us with a 360-degree view of threats within our organization before they even arise."

Movie And Video Production
Complete Self-Assessment Guide

Table of Contents

About The Art of Service

The Art of Service, Business Process Architects since 2000, is dedicated to helping stakeholders achieve excellence.

Defining, designing, creating, and implementing a process to solve a stakeholders challenge or meet an objective is the most valuable role... In EVERY group, company, organization and department.

Unless you're talking a one-time, single-use project, there should be a process. Whether that process is managed and implemented by humans, AI, or a combination of the two, it needs to be designed by someone with a complex enough perspective to ask the right questions.

Someone capable of asking the right questions and step back and say, 'What are we really trying to accomplish here? And is there a different way to look at it?'

With The Art of Service's Self-Assessments, we empower people who can do just that — whether their title is marketer, entrepreneur, manager, salesperson, consultant, Business Process Manager, executive assistant, IT Manager, CIO etc... —they are the people who rule the future. They are people who watch the process as it happens, and ask the right questions to make the process work better.

Contact us when you need any support with this Self-Assessment and any help with templates, blue-prints and examples of standard documents you might need:

https://theartofservice.com
support@theartofservice.com

Included Resources - how to access

Included with your purchase of the book is the Movie And Video

Production Self-Assessment Spreadsheet Dashboard which contains all questions and Self-Assessment areas and auto-generates insights, graphs, and project RACI planning - all with examples to get you started right away.

How? Simply send an email to
access@theartofservice.com
with this books' title in the subject to get the Movie And Video Production Self Assessment Tool right away.

The auto reply will guide you further, you will then receive the following contents with New and Updated specific criteria:

- The latest quick edition of the book in PDF
- The latest complete edition of the book in PDF, which criteria correspond to the criteria in...
- The Self-Assessment Excel Dashboard, and...
- Example pre-filled Self-Assessment Excel Dashboard to get familiar with results generation
- In-depth specific Checklists covering the topic
- Project management checklists and templates to assist with implementation

INCLUDES LIFETIME SELF ASSESSMENT UPDATES

Every self assessment comes with Lifetime Updates and Lifetime Free Updated Books. Lifetime Updates is an industry-first feature which allows you to receive verified self assessment updates, ensuring you always have the most accurate information at your fingertips.

Get it now- you will be glad you did - do it now, before you forget.

Send an email to **access@theartofservice.com** with this books' title in the subject to get the Movie And Video Production Self Assessment Tool right away.

Purpose of this Self-Assessment

This Self-Assessment has been developed to improve understanding of the requirements and elements of Movie And Video Production, based on best practices and standards in business process architecture, design and quality management.

It is designed to allow for a rapid Self-Assessment to determine how closely existing management practices and procedures correspond to the elements of the Self-Assessment.

The criteria of requirements and elements of Movie And Video Production have been rephrased in the format of a Self-Assessment questionnaire, with a seven-criterion scoring system, as explained in this document.

In this format, even with limited background knowledge of Movie And Video Production, a manager can quickly review existing operations to determine how they measure up to the standards. This in turn can serve as the starting point of a 'gap analysis' to identify management tools or system elements that might usefully be implemented in the organization to help improve overall performance.

How to use the Self-Assessment

On the following pages are a series of questions to identify to what extent your Movie And Video Production initiative is complete in comparison to the requirements set in standards.

To facilitate answering the questions, there is a space in front of each question to enter a score on a scale of '1' to '5'.

1 Strongly Disagree

2 Disagree

3 Neutral

4 Agree

5 Strongly Agree

Read the question and rate it with the following in front of mind:

'In my belief, the answer to this question is clearly defined'.

There are two ways in which you can choose to interpret this statement;

1. how aware are you that the answer to the question is clearly defined
2. for more in-depth analysis you can choose to gather evidence and confirm the answer to the question. This obviously will take more time, most Self-Assessment users opt for the first way to interpret the question and dig deeper later on based on the outcome of the overall Self-Assessment.

A score of '1' would mean that the answer is not clear at all, where a '5' would mean the answer is crystal clear and defined. Leave emtpy when the question is not applicable or you don't want to answer it, you can skip it without affecting your score. Write your score in the space provided.

After you have responded to all the appropriate statements in each section, compute your average score for that section, using the formula provided, and round to the nearest tenth. Then transfer to the corresponding spoke in the Movie And Video Production Scorecard on the second next page of the Self-Assessment.

Your completed Movie And Video Production Scorecard will give you a clear presentation of which Movie And Video Production areas need attention.

Movie And Video Production Scorecard Example

Example of how the finalized Scorecard can look like:

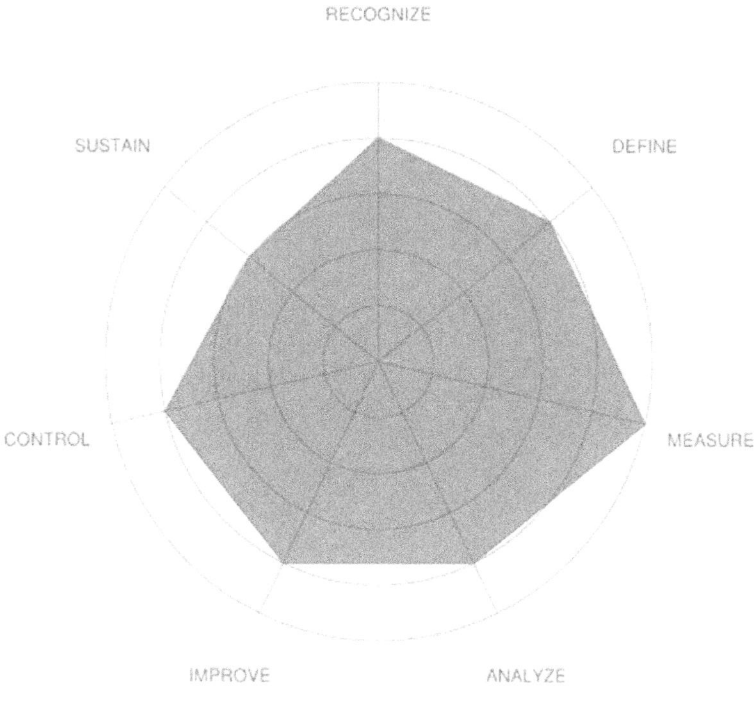

Movie And Video Production Scorecard

Your Scores:

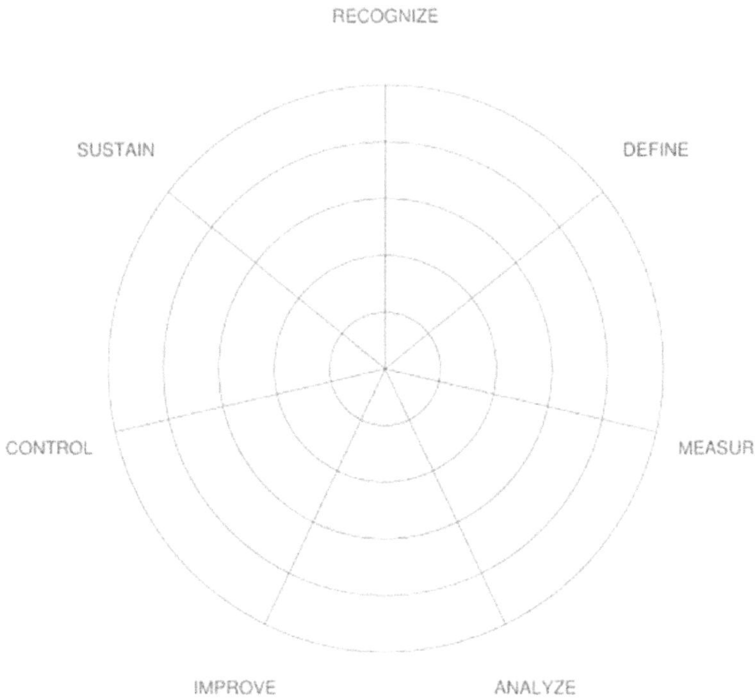

BEGINNING OF THE SELF-ASSESSMENT:

CRITERION #1: RECOGNIZE

INTENT: Be aware of the need for change. Recognize that there is an unfavorable variation, problem or symptom.

In my belief, the answer to this question is clearly defined:

5 Strongly Agree

4 Agree

3 Neutral

2 Disagree

1 Strongly Disagree

1. What components of the system model affect the problem?
<--- Score

2. What would happen if Movie and Video Production weren't done?
<--- Score

3. What are the existing initiatives or methods of

identifying security threats and attacks?
<--- Score

4. Do you have the most efficient form of asset utilisation to meet the service need?
<--- Score

5. Why, if there are so many problems with the SDLC model, is it still being used?
<--- Score

6. What Movie and Video Production coordination do you need?
<--- Score

7. Why would there be need to manually modify generated code in a software project?
<--- Score

8. Who else hopes to benefit from it?
<--- Score

9. What are the most efficient forms of asset utilisation and ownership to meet service needs?
<--- Score

10. Why do you need the customer domain model separate from the handy ORM at all?
<--- Score

11. Should you hold the asset for future service needs?
<--- Score

12. Can agents/branches provide enough liquidity to meet program needs?

<--- Score

13. What do you need for a context management system?
<--- Score

14. What steps does the industry need to take to change the business model?
<--- Score

15. Are employees recognized for desired behaviors?
<--- Score

16. What ongoing efforts and resources are need after a system is up and running?
<--- Score

17. What are the stakeholder objectives to be achieved with Movie and Video Production?
<--- Score

18. Who do you need to work with to make the model work?
<--- Score

19. How are the Movie and Video Production's objectives aligned to the group's overall stakeholder strategy?
<--- Score

20. Is it identifiable as a requirement?
<--- Score

21. Does Movie and Video Production create potential expectations in other areas that need to be recognized and considered?

<--- Score

22. As a sponsor, customer or management, how important is it to meet goals, objectives?
<--- Score

23. Think about the people you identified for your Movie and Video Production project and the project responsibilities you would assign to them, what kind of training do you think they would need to perform these responsibilities effectively?
<--- Score

24. How many posts does it take to solve problems, and what is the duration of the considerations?
<--- Score

25. What are the benefits, challenges, and supply chain metrics of each identified model?
<--- Score

26. Who needs to know?
<--- Score

27. Are there issues associated with multi vendor supply of IoT devices in terms of a common cybersecurity approach?
<--- Score

28. What are issues related to strategic business alignment model in context of information technology?
<--- Score

29. What situation(s) led to this Movie and Video

Production Self Assessment?
<--- Score

30. Which cloud deployment model seems best fit to your needs?
<--- Score

31. What do you need to start doing?
<--- Score

32. Have you identified one or more mitigations for each threat?
<--- Score

33. Does all the resources need to be at onsite or an onsite and offshore model will work?
<--- Score

34. How do you identify, specify and categorize the platform independent models?
<--- Score

35. How do you find security issues in your applications and systems?
<--- Score

36. What are the expected benefits of Movie and Video Production to the stakeholder?
<--- Score

37. Which information and material flows does is it need?
<--- Score

38. How are you going to measure success?
<--- Score

39. Are information needs at operational nodes met by systems available?
<--- Score

40. What problems are you facing and how do you consider Movie and Video Production will circumvent those obstacles?
<--- Score

41. How are training requirements identified?
<--- Score

42. Do you actually need a shared service or is there a better delivery model?
<--- Score

43. What is the recognized need?
<--- Score

44. What does Movie and Video Production success mean to the stakeholders?
<--- Score

45. Are there any specific expectations or concerns about the Movie and Video Production team, Movie and Video Production itself?
<--- Score

46. How much are sponsors, customers, partners, stakeholders involved in Movie and Video Production? In other words, what are the risks, if Movie and Video Production does not deliver successfully?
<--- Score

Add up total points for this section:

_____ = Total points for this section

Divided by: ______ (number of statements answered) = ______ Average score for this section

Transfer your score to the Movie and Video Production Index at the beginning of the Self-Assessment.

CRITERION #2: DEFINE:

INTENT: Formulate the stakeholder problem. Define the problem, needs and objectives.

In my belief, the answer to this question is clearly defined:

5 Strongly Agree

4 Agree

3 Neutral

2 Disagree

1 Strongly Disagree

1. Is the team adequately staffed with the desired cross-functionality? If not, what additional resources are available to the team?
<--- Score

2. What is the role of the requirements in software verification?
<--- Score

3. Can the required numbers of different staff with the required competences be modelled?
<--- Score

4. Does the component reject illegal messages, even when syntactically well formed, based on dynamic context?
<--- Score

5. Are different versions of process maps needed to account for the different types of inputs?
<--- Score

6. Is there regularly 100% attendance at the team meetings? If not, have appointed substitutes attended to preserve cross-functionality and full representation?
<--- Score

7. What level of channel integration is required?
<--- Score

8. Does the team have regular meetings?
<--- Score

9. Is a fully trained team formed, supported, and committed to work on the Movie and Video Production improvements?
<--- Score

10. Is the requirement set better suited to be combined into a single requirement?
<--- Score

11. Is there a completed, verified, and validated high-level 'as is' (not 'should be' or 'could be') stakeholder

process map?
<--- Score

12. What business areas are most stable and least likely to require change?
<--- Score

13. Has the Movie and Video Production work been fairly and/or equitably divided and delegated among team members who are qualified and capable to perform the work? Has everyone contributed?
<--- Score

14. What about performance requirements / resources?
<--- Score

15. Has anyone else (internal or external to the group) attempted to solve this problem or a similar one before? If so, what knowledge can be leveraged from these previous efforts?
<--- Score

16. Will team members perform Movie and Video Production work when assigned and in a timely fashion?
<--- Score

17. Are the Movie and Video Production requirements testable?
<--- Score

18. Who is gathering information?
<--- Score

19. What customer feedback methods were used to

solicit their input?
<--- Score

20. What are the boundaries of the scope? What is in bounds and what is not? What is the start point? What is the stop point?
<--- Score

21. What setup is required before a precast modeling can happen?
<--- Score

22. What is the scope of Movie and Video Production?
<--- Score

23. How much do regulatory requirements vary between the markets?
<--- Score

24. Has a high-level 'as is' process map been completed, verified and validated?
<--- Score

25. What knowledge or experience is required?
<--- Score

26. What are the Roles and Responsibilities for each team member and its leadership? Where is this documented?
<--- Score

27. How experienced are you with gathering requirements?
<--- Score

28. What is a worst-case scenario for losses?

<--- Score

29. Has the improvement team collected the 'voice of the customer' (obtained feedback – qualitative and quantitative)?
<--- Score

30. What critical content must be communicated – who, what, when, where, and how?
<--- Score

31. Has everyone on the team, including the team leaders, been properly trained?
<--- Score

32. What constraints exist that might impact the team?
<--- Score

33. Do the problem and goal statements meet the SMART criteria (specific, measurable, attainable, relevant, and time-bound)?
<--- Score

34. Is there a requirement to maintain a minimum balance to keep the account open/pay monthly service fees?
<--- Score

35. Which of the requirements can be reasonably implemented in the next iteration?
<--- Score

36. Who are the Movie and Video Production improvement team members, including Management Leads and Coaches?

<--- Score

37. Did the viable systems model at any point require the use of authority and obedience?
<--- Score

38. What are the rough order estimates on cost savings/opportunities that Movie and Video Production brings?
<--- Score

39. Does the requirement conflict with others?
<--- Score

40. What are the dynamics of the communication plan?
<--- Score

41. Is the Movie and Video Production scope manageable?
<--- Score

42. How will the Movie and Video Production team and the group measure complete success of Movie and Video Production?
<--- Score

43. Do you provide tools to support the defined model?
<--- Score

44. Is it physically possible to meet the requirements?
<--- Score

45. Has/have the customer(s) been identified?

<--- Score

46. Are there different segments of customers?
<--- Score

47. Do the requirements trace to test cases?
<--- Score

48. When is/was the Movie and Video Production start date?
<--- Score

49. What is there about strategic business alignment model in the context of information technology?
<--- Score

50. If substitutes have been appointed, have they been briefed on the Movie and Video Production goals and received regular communications as to the progress to date?
<--- Score

51. Is the team equipped with available and reliable resources?
<--- Score

52. Is the improvement team aware of the different versions of a process: what they think it is vs. what it actually is vs. what it should be vs. what it could be?
<--- Score

53. What key stakeholder process output measure(s) does Movie and Video Production leverage and how?
<--- Score

54. How and when will the baselines be defined?
<--- Score

55. Do organization acquisition policy and guidance allow for changing requirements?
<--- Score

56. How did the Movie and Video Production manager receive input to the development of a Movie and Video Production improvement plan and the estimated completion dates/times of each activity?
<--- Score

57. What are the compelling stakeholder reasons for embarking on Movie and Video Production?
<--- Score

58. What specifically is the problem? Where does it occur? When does it occur? What is its extent?
<--- Score

59. Are team charters developed?
<--- Score

60. Will team members regularly document their Movie and Video Production work?
<--- Score

61. How often are the team meetings?
<--- Score

62. Is Movie and Video Production linked to key stakeholder goals and objectives?
<--- Score

63. Is full participation by members in regularly held

team meetings guaranteed?
<--- Score

64. Are there any constraints known that bear on the ability to perform Movie and Video Production work? How is the team addressing them?
<--- Score

65. When is the estimated completion date?
<--- Score

66. When are meeting minutes sent out? Who is on the distribution list?
<--- Score

67. How will variation in the actual durations of each activity be dealt with to ensure that the expected Movie and Video Production results are met?
<--- Score

68. Is the current 'as is' process being followed? If not, what are the discrepancies?
<--- Score

69. Is data collected and displayed to better understand customer(s) critical needs and requirements.
<--- Score

70. Are customer(s) identified and segmented according to their different needs and requirements?
<--- Score

71. Is there a Movie and Video Production management charter, including stakeholder case, problem and goal statements, scope, milestones, roles

and responsibilities, communication plan?
<--- Score

72. What is the scope of capability management?
<--- Score

73. What information do you gather?
<--- Score

74. Is there a critical path to deliver Movie and Video Production results?
<--- Score

75. Is Movie and Video Production currently on schedule according to the plan?
<--- Score

76. Is the Movie and Video Production scope complete and appropriately sized?
<--- Score

77. Has a team charter been developed and communicated?
<--- Score

78. How does the Movie and Video Production manager ensure against scope creep?
<--- Score

79. Is it the case that models only represent services?
<--- Score

80. What scope do you want your strategy to cover?
<--- Score

81. What are the main reported benefits of strategic business alignment model in the context of information technology?
<--- Score

82. How performance is measured in the supply chain context?
<--- Score

83. How is the service delivery area of the coordinated services approach defined?
<--- Score

84. Is it clearly defined in and to your organization what you do?
<--- Score

85. Are stakeholder processes mapped?
<--- Score

86. How do you model the functional requirements for a software system?
<--- Score

87. Are approval levels defined for contracts and supplements to contracts?
<--- Score

88. Who defines (or who defined) the rules and roles?
<--- Score

89. Is the network coverage strong enough for the transaction to occur when required?
<--- Score

90. Have the customer needs been translated into

specific, measurable requirements? How?
<--- Score

91. What would be the goal or target for a Movie and Video Production's improvement team?
<--- Score

92. Has a project plan, Gantt chart, or similar been developed/completed?
<--- Score

93. Has the direction changed at all during the course of Movie and Video Production? If so, when did it change and why?
<--- Score

94. What is the scope of the Movie and Video Production effort?
<--- Score

95. How do you keep key subject matter experts in the loop?
<--- Score

96. Are customers identified and high impact areas defined?
<--- Score

97. Does component/service support requirement?
<--- Score

98. Is there a completed SIPOC representation, describing the Suppliers, Inputs, Process, Outputs, and Customers?
<--- Score

99. What support is required for doing service oriented enterprise architecture?
<--- Score

100. How is the team tracking and documenting its work?
<--- Score

101. Is the team formed and are team leaders (Coaches and Management Leads) assigned?
<--- Score

102. Do you all define Movie and Video Production in the same way?
<--- Score

103. How was the 'as is' process map developed, reviewed, verified and validated?
<--- Score

104. Is the team sponsored by a champion or stakeholder leader?
<--- Score

105. Are improvement team members fully trained on Movie and Video Production?
<--- Score

106. Is the work to date meeting requirements?
<--- Score

Add up total points for this section:
_____ = Total points for this section

Divided by: ______ (number of

statements answered) = ______
Average score for this section

Transfer your score to the Movie and Video Production Index at the beginning of the Self-Assessment.

CRITERION #3: MEASURE:

INTENT: Gather the correct data. Measure the current performance and evolution of the situation.

In my belief, the answer to this question is clearly defined:

5 Strongly Agree

4 Agree

3 Neutral

2 Disagree

1 Strongly Disagree

1. Do you change the focus of current assets to meet service need?
<--- Score

2. Have you found any 'ground fruit' or 'low-hanging fruit' for immediate remedies to the gap in performance?
<--- Score

3. What are the uncertainties surrounding estimates of impact?
<--- Score

4. Are process variation components displayed/ communicated using suitable charts, graphs, plots?
<--- Score

5. What users will be impacted?
<--- Score

6. Are the impacts of mitigations aligned to the business goals and priorities?
<--- Score

7. Which analysis techniques derive system models from existing system or discovery prototypes?
<--- Score

8. What causes mismanagement?
<--- Score

9. What are your key Movie and Video Production organizational performance measures, including key short and longer-term financial measures?
<--- Score

10. What is the cost of rework?
<--- Score

11. How to cause the change?
<--- Score

12. How can attained business agility be measured in completed SOA projects?
<--- Score

13. How will the asset impact service costs?
<--- Score

14. What particular quality tools did the team find helpful in establishing measurements?
<--- Score

15. Does the service fit your prioritization model?
<--- Score

16. What kind of analytics data will be gathered?
<--- Score

17. What are the costs of delaying Movie and Video Production action?
<--- Score

18. Is long term and short term variability accounted for?
<--- Score

19. How is progress measured?
<--- Score

20. How do you control and measure services and service providers?
<--- Score

21. Does your organization systematically track and analyze outcomes related for accountability and quality improvement?
<--- Score

22. Are you able to realize any cost savings?
<--- Score

23. Why a Movie and Video Production focus?
<--- Score

24. What is the cost of the process compared to the benefits of its results?
<--- Score

25. How do you control the overall costs of your work processes?
<--- Score

26. How do you measure the worth of an architects performance?
<--- Score

27. Is the team working from a prioritized backlog to provide frequent software deliveries?
<--- Score

28. Are there enough non financial benefits to justify the business case in the absence of cost benefit?
<--- Score

29. What are your organizations priorities?
<--- Score

30. What are the key input variables? What are the key process variables? What are the key output variables?
<--- Score

31. What is the cost of the request regarding dollars and resources?
<--- Score

32. What key measures identified indicate the performance of the stakeholder process?
<--- Score

33. How do you measure future readiness of an operating model?
<--- Score

34. Is component/service cost within estimated cost?
<--- Score

35. Is there a Performance Baseline?
<--- Score

36. Are you using production system predictive analytics to feed into the knowledge base?
<--- Score

37. What is the impact of implied scenarios on reliability?
<--- Score

38. How has it impacted you, your organization, your operations and the impact on people and loneliness and isolation?
<--- Score

39. Is data collected on key measures that were identified?
<--- Score

40. Are high impact defects defined and identified in the stakeholder process?
<--- Score

41. Do you have an issue in getting priority?
<--- Score

42. What impact does it have on older people?
<--- Score

43. What do you measure and why?
<--- Score

44. Why should you analyze security ceremonies?
<--- Score

45. Where is it measured?
<--- Score

46. When is Root Cause Analysis Required?
<--- Score

47. Was a data collection plan established?
<--- Score

48. Who pays the cost?
<--- Score

49. What exactly should a source code analyzer do?
<--- Score

50. Does your organization prioritize the scope and frequency of validation activities?
<--- Score

51. Does management have the right priorities among projects?
<--- Score

52. How will the new shared service model impact current operations?
<--- Score

53. Have you made assumptions about the shape of the future, particularly its impact on your customers and competitors?
<--- Score

54. Are there any models that support competitor analysis where quality is compared?
<--- Score

55. What are the expected concept weights or system level weight impacts?
<--- Score

56. Who participated in the data collection for measurements?
<--- Score

57. Do you effectively measure and reward individual and team performance?
<--- Score

58. How long to keep data and how to manage retention costs?
<--- Score

59. Do you believe SWOT analysis of the customer is a critical step to understand the business model?
<--- Score

60. How well is your enterprise architecture positively impacting products and business strategy?

<--- Score

61. What data was collected (past, present, future/ ongoing)?
<--- Score

62. How large is the gap between current performance and the customer-specified (goal) performance?
<--- Score

63. How frequently do you track Movie and Video Production measures?
<--- Score

64. Are you making use of up to date predictive analysis engines?
<--- Score

65. How easy is it for someone else on the cost team to use the model?
<--- Score

66. What is the Movie and Video Production business impact?
<--- Score

67. Which costs should be taken into account?
<--- Score

68. Are key measures identified and agreed upon?
<--- Score

69. How can a Movie and Video Production test verify your ideas or assumptions?
<--- Score

70. Does your organization use the models/ software to analyze/manage risks?
<--- Score

71. Is a solid data collection plan established that includes measurement systems analysis?
<--- Score

72. What are your customers expectations and measures?
<--- Score

73. How do well established innovate the business model to explore data analytics value?
<--- Score

74. What are the agreed upon definitions of the high impact areas, defect(s), unit(s), and opportunities that will figure into the process capability metrics?
<--- Score

75. How would the time to maximum effect of a feedback message be measured?
<--- Score

76. What charts has the team used to display the components of variation in the process?
<--- Score

77. What has the team done to assure the stability and accuracy of the measurement process?
<--- Score

78. Is Process Variation Displayed/Communicated?
<--- Score

79. What are the quickest and the most cost effective way for adapting systems with new technologies?
<--- Score

80. How does the choice of a procurement operating model impact results delivered?
<--- Score

81. Does your analysis indicate any problems with the relevance of the basic stable process model assumptions?
<--- Score

82. What are the most important costs when operating the business model?
<--- Score

83. What should be prioritized as you review alternate locations?
<--- Score

84. How can business agility be measured in completed SOA projects?
<--- Score

85. Do you have one cost model for all services or separate cost models for multiple services?
<--- Score

86. Why is a scenario used to analysing external environment?
<--- Score

87. How do you measure the system quality?

<--- Score

88. Is data collection planned and executed?
<--- Score

89. Is key measure data collection planned and executed, process variation displayed and communicated and performance baselined?
<--- Score

90. How do you prevent mis-estimating cost?
<--- Score

91. What sort of organizational and measurement infrastructure is necessary to calculate the worth?
<--- Score

92. What is the cost model of the solution?
<--- Score

93. How is performance of the system measured?
<--- Score

94. What is the Total Cost of Ownership of and ASP as compared to traditional models?
<--- Score

95. Are advantages based on analytics and modeling potentially sustainable?
<--- Score

Add up total points for this section:
_____ = Total points for this section

Divided by: ______ (number of statements answered) = ______

Average score for this section

Transfer your score to the Movie and Video Production Index at the beginning of the Self-Assessment.

CRITERION #4: ANALYZE:

INTENT: Analyze causes, assumptions and hypotheses.

In my belief, the answer to this question is clearly defined:

5 Strongly Agree

4 Agree

3 Neutral

2 Disagree

1 Strongly Disagree

1. What steps were involved in designing the database/warehouse?
<--- Score

2. Which are the main processes of the enterprises?
<--- Score

3. What transient or persistent data is inherently meaningful to the system?
<--- Score

4. What tools were used to narrow the list of possible causes?
<--- Score

5. What is the purpose of the model database?
<--- Score

6. How can reaction securely transfer data?
<--- Score

7. What is the research method for validation process?
<--- Score

8. How can runtime data be used to ensure that there is an accurate model of the manufacturing system?
<--- Score

9. Does an architecture support domain driven design?
<--- Score

10. What tools were used to generate the list of possible causes?
<--- Score

11. How do you spot opportunities for innovation?
<--- Score

12. Who will facilitate the team and process?
<--- Score

13. Is there any way to speed up the process?
<--- Score

14. What are your key performance measures or indicators and in-process measures for the control and improvement of your Movie and Video Production processes?
<--- Score

15. What actual processing and response speeds are required and what is acceptable?
<--- Score

16. Was a detailed process map created to amplify critical steps of the 'as is' stakeholder process?
<--- Score

17. Has your organization consolidated or will consolidate the work/data centers or networks?
<--- Score

18. What are the disruptive Movie and Video Production technologies that enable your organization to radically change your business processes?
<--- Score

19. Do you need a high level view when considering data models with management?
<--- Score

20. What qualifications are necessary?
<--- Score

21. What quality tools were used to get through the analyze phase?
<--- Score

22. Has a process supporting innovation activity been modelled on the platform?
<--- Score

23. What were the financial benefits resulting from any 'ground fruit or low-hanging fruit' (quick fixes)?
<--- Score

24. What are the data center services that you currently provide?
<--- Score

25. What is the difference between synchronous and asynchronous processing?
<--- Score

26. How accessible is the information used in the process?
<--- Score

27. Should you validate data at each node?
<--- Score

28. Does the model implementation process use similar data as used in the model development process?
<--- Score

29. What is the proper classification marking for the input data and the resulting model?
<--- Score

30. Does existing market data indicate that markets should be able to respond to an increase in demand?
<--- Score

31. Are the sensor models developed based on real driving data?
<--- Score

32. Are you set up to manage process change?
<--- Score

33. What are the best opportunities for value improvement?
<--- Score

34. How has the Movie and Video Production data been gathered?
<--- Score

35. How does your organization work throughout the levels to improve its processes?
<--- Score

36. How is the system of goals represented is the process modeled goal oriented?
<--- Score

37. What did the team gain from developing a sub-process map?
<--- Score

38. Does your organization have data that show is improved quality of products and/or services?
<--- Score

39. What are the Movie and Video Production design outputs?
<--- Score

40. How do you secure time critical data transfer from external resources?
<--- Score

41. What is business process modeling?
<--- Score

42. Why you need client server model for data base applications?
<--- Score

43. What drives efficiency of service delivery?
<--- Score

44. Are measurements implemented which indicate level of output and effectiveness?
<--- Score

45. Where can you get qualified talent today?
<--- Score

46. How can cooperative work tools support dynamic group processes?
<--- Score

47. Did any additional data need to be collected?
<--- Score

48. Is the process primarily manual or automated?
<--- Score

49. Which data is stored in the core server?
<--- Score

50. Are there models of good practice which demonstrate the potential of data sharing?

<--- Score

51. How to innovate successful circular economy driven business models?
<--- Score

52. Identify an operational issue in your organization, for example, could a particular task be done more quickly or more efficiently by Movie and Video Production?
<--- Score

53. Are there any non default master or model database objects?
<--- Score

54. Were any designed experiments used to generate additional insight into the data analysis?
<--- Score

55. How do availability, response time and capacity fit into your output input model?
<--- Score

56. How timely is the end to end process?
<--- Score

57. What is arranged or will be arranged to maintain the single data point model?
<--- Score

58. Do you see the processes that move data from one data store to another?
<--- Score

59. What does the data say about the performance of

the stakeholder process?
<--- Score

60. Is data and process analysis, root cause analysis and quantifying the gap/opportunity in place?
<--- Score

61. How do you build a simple, maintainable, and adaptable transformation process?
<--- Score

62. What are evaluation criteria for the output?
<--- Score

63. How do you ensure that the Movie and Video Production opportunity is realistic?
<--- Score

64. What qualifications are needed?
<--- Score

65. What is been the process of expanding into that enterprise sales model?
<--- Score

66. Is it safe to move key business and financial processes to SaaS from your premises?
<--- Score

67. What are the processes for audit reporting and management?
<--- Score

68. Were there any improvement opportunities identified from the process analysis?
<--- Score

69. Is the Movie and Video Production process severely broken such that a re-design is necessary?
<--- Score

70. How is data used for program management and improvement?
<--- Score

71. What is the cost of poor quality as supported by the team's analysis?
<--- Score

72. Is there a process for revalidation of credentials?
<--- Score

73. Are databases of any use in modern geo services?
<--- Score

74. Is a canonical data model in place?
<--- Score

75. How do you bring cloud computing models and technologies into your datacenter?
<--- Score

76. Were Pareto charts (or similar) used to portray the 'heavy hitters' (or key sources of variation)?
<--- Score

77. Do you know what happens to all the data associated with an account when its terminated?
<--- Score

78. Are you using an automated risk management process?
<--- Score

79. What will drive Movie and Video Production change?
<--- Score

80. What is business process modeling software?
<--- Score

81. What are your best practices for minimizing Movie and Video Production project risk, while demonstrating incremental value and quick wins throughout the Movie and Video Production project lifecycle?
<--- Score

82. Is there a documented process for acquisition?
<--- Score

83. Is etl software needed to build a model driven dss?
<--- Score

84. What is the proper classification marking for input data and the resulting model?
<--- Score

85. Is there a strict change management process?
<--- Score

86. What is the goal of a software process model?
<--- Score

87. What systems/processes must you excel at?

<--- Score

88. Is the risk management process continually improving?
<--- Score

89. Is the modeled manufacturing process complete from material lead time to final inspection?
<--- Score

90. How easy was it for you to understand the data source model?
<--- Score

91. Do you have the right governance process and operating model in place to ensure success?
<--- Score

92. When should a process be art not science?
<--- Score

93. What data need to be exchanged to implement the threads?
<--- Score

94. How will the data be checked for quality?
<--- Score

95. What sdlc model is most frequently associated with cloud development processes?
<--- Score

96. Does the data need to be stored at each subsequent visit or evaluation?
<--- Score

97. How accurate is the information used in the process?
<--- Score

98. How was the detailed process map generated, verified, and validated?
<--- Score

99. How has the model of process improvement evolved?
<--- Score

100. Is the performance gap determined?
<--- Score

101. How do you locate the process that is using a specific network address?
<--- Score

102. Is there a documented process for software development?
<--- Score

103. What Movie and Video Production data will be collected?
<--- Score

104. What are the revised rough estimates of the financial savings/opportunity for Movie and Video Production improvements?
<--- Score

105. Which customer journeys drive the largest number of calls?
<--- Score

106. How should opportunities be assessed, rated and presented?
<--- Score

107. Which security mechanism you need for data/ communication?
<--- Score

108. How easy was it for you to comment on the data source model?
<--- Score

109. Is your data model in good shape?
<--- Score

110. How important is the data source model to give your requirements?
<--- Score

111. Do you model data protection aspects, as security measures or anonymization?
<--- Score

112. Is there an opportunity for distributed organizations to skip centrally located staffing models and move to more virtual shared services?
<--- Score

113. What are you doing to improve your innovation process?
<--- Score

114. Where is Movie and Video Production data gathered?
<--- Score

115. Are your outputs consistent?
<--- Score

116. Is there a sufficient amount of one data to perform reasoning on?
<--- Score

117. What is a model driven engineering?
<--- Score

118. Have any additional benefits been identified that will result from closing all or most of the gaps?
<--- Score

119. Does the model use information from other data systems?
<--- Score

120. What were the crucial 'moments of truth' on the process map?
<--- Score

121. Is the gap/opportunity displayed and communicated in financial terms?
<--- Score

122. What is maturity of producer development process?
<--- Score

123. Is the required Movie and Video Production data gathered?
<--- Score

124. What is a software process model?

<--- Score

125. Which are the processes to be supported by the system?
<--- Score

126. How best to leverage AI and other opportunities?
<--- Score

127. How to successfully implement the metadata driven workflow model?
<--- Score

128. Is critical data stored off site?
<--- Score

129. What conclusions were drawn from the team's data collection and analysis? How did the team reach these conclusions?
<--- Score

130. How will corresponding data be collected?
<--- Score

131. What Movie and Video Production data should be managed?
<--- Score

132. Why use systems engineering leads and practitioners as primary data sources?
<--- Score

133. Do you see where all the data goes and who uses it?
<--- Score

134. Who gets your output?
<--- Score

135. Was a cause-and-effect diagram used to explore the different types of causes (or sources of variation)?
<--- Score

136. Does it use any configuration or system files to generate the output?
<--- Score

137. Are policies, processes, and staffing appropriate for supporting the model?
<--- Score

138. What is a common problem overlooked in data modeling when dealing with multiple data sources?
<--- Score

139. Did any value-added analysis or 'lean thinking' take place to identify some of the gaps shown on the 'as is' process map?
<--- Score

140. Have the problem and goal statements been updated to reflect the additional knowledge gained from the analyze phase?
<--- Score

141. What, would be an alternative for the business model innovation process?
<--- Score

Add up total points for this section:

_____ = Total points for this section

Divided by: ______ (number of statements answered) = ______ Average score for this section

Transfer your score to the Movie and Video Production Index at the beginning of the Self-Assessment.

CRITERION #5: IMPROVE:

INTENT: Develop a practical solution. Innovate, establish and test the solution and to measure the results.

In my belief, the answer to this question is clearly defined:

5 Strongly Agree

4 Agree

3 Neutral

2 Disagree

1 Strongly Disagree

1. Does your organization use modeling software to identify the characteristics of optimal customers?
<--- Score

2. Why is it important to software development?
<--- Score

3. What assumptions are made about the solution and

approach?
<--- Score

4. Does a good decision guarantee a good outcome?
<--- Score

5. How is continuous improvement applied to risk management?
<--- Score

6. Is the team identifying risk in production?
<--- Score

7. Are board reports tailored to your organizations size, complexity, risks, and model usage?
<--- Score

8. What tools were most useful during the improve phase?
<--- Score

9. What lessons, if any, from a pilot were incorporated into the design of the full-scale solution?
<--- Score

10. How do developers perceive and interpret the concept of privacy in the daily work?
<--- Score

11. Are improved process ('should be') maps modified based on pilot data and analysis?
<--- Score

12. Does your organization develop innovation competence as a by product of service delivery?
<--- Score

13. How many detection models have you developed?
<--- Score

14. How does the Service Design project model develop?
<--- Score

15. What other mitigation methodologies exist when developing software, to conceive secure systems?
<--- Score

16. Are the best solutions selected?
<--- Score

17. How does the solution remove the key sources of issues discovered in the analyze phase?
<--- Score

18. Is the Movie and Video Production solution sustainable?
<--- Score

19. Do you have the optimal project management team structure?
<--- Score

20. What is the optimal delivery model?
<--- Score

21. Which criteria are required in the service supplier evaluation model?
<--- Score

22. At what point will vulnerability assessments be performed once Movie and Video Production is put into production (e.g., ongoing Risk Management after implementation)?
<--- Score

23. When did you decide to initiate innovation of the existing business model?
<--- Score

24. Does your organization have an effective and efficient integrated risk and control model?
<--- Score

25. Are risk management tasks balanced centrally and locally?
<--- Score

26. What models are within the scope of model risk management?
<--- Score

27. Does your team test customers /users privacy aspects during software development?
<--- Score

28. Is model risk being quantified systematically?
<--- Score

29. Is pilot data collected and analyzed?
<--- Score

30. Is there a close partnership between the developers, program managers, customers, and contractors?
<--- Score

31. How do you decide on a sourcing strategy for services?
<--- Score

32. What is Movie and Video Production's impact on utilizing the best solution(s)?
<--- Score

33. Does your organization follow any model for evaluating supplier performance?
<--- Score

34. Is a contingency plan established?
<--- Score

35. What tools were used to tap into the creativity and encourage 'outside the box' thinking?
<--- Score

36. How can mbse help you make better decisions?
<--- Score

37. Is the optimal solution selected based on testing and analysis?
<--- Score

38. Are there any constraints (technical, political, cultural, or otherwise) that would inhibit certain solutions?
<--- Score

39. Have you changed anything in your system as a result?
<--- Score

40. When does the matched model methodology give the same result as hedonic methodology?
<--- Score

41. Are new and improved process ('should be') maps developed?
<--- Score

42. How do the models help you evaluate an individuals or organizations ability to do that?
<--- Score

43. Does it cover all the security decisions you made?
<--- Score

44. Which kind of risk sharing business models are most often used?
<--- Score

45. What tools were used to evaluate the potential solutions?
<--- Score

46. Are the key business and technology risks being managed?
<--- Score

47. How many custom correlation rules and detection models have you developed?
<--- Score

48. Is a solution implementation plan established, including schedule/work breakdown structure, resources, risk management plan, cost/budget, and control plan?

<--- Score

49. Is there a small-scale pilot for proposed improvement(s)? What conclusions were drawn from the outcomes of a pilot?
<--- Score

50. Is there a shared understanding of value among the team, program, and organization?
<--- Score

51. Who are the Movie and Video Production decision-makers?
<--- Score

52. How can the phases of Movie and Video Production development be identified?
<--- Score

53. Is there any other Movie and Video Production solution?
<--- Score

54. Is the program facilitating improved access to generalist and specialist services?
<--- Score

55. For estimation problems, how do you develop an estimation statement?
<--- Score

56. Are your developers working with models and code?
<--- Score

57. What specifications are required for the first

development cycle?
<--- Score

58. What can be done to improve local service accountability and effectiveness?
<--- Score

59. What is the team's contingency plan for potential problems occurring in implementation?
<--- Score

60. How will you know that a change is an improvement?
<--- Score

61. How will the team or the process owner(s) monitor the implementation plan to see that it is working as intended?
<--- Score

62. What were the underlying assumptions on the cost-benefit analysis?
<--- Score

63. Was a pilot designed for the proposed solution(s)?
<--- Score

64. Who manages supplier risk management in your organization?
<--- Score

65. Are procedures documented for managing Movie and Video Production risks?
<--- Score

66. What steps are taken to understand the

software before reuse/update/upgrade?
<--- Score

67. What attendant changes will need to be made to ensure that the solution is successful?
<--- Score

68. Are you involving the system owners in assessing risk?
<--- Score

69. Do you know some models/softwares that are used to manage risk?
<--- Score

70. What alternative responses are available to manage risk?
<--- Score

71. Are the most efficient solutions problem-specific?
<--- Score

72. What specifications are required for the second development cycle?
<--- Score

73. How will the group know that the solution worked?
<--- Score

74. Which aspects of the risk modeling lifecycle have you started modernizing, if any?
<--- Score

75. Have you considered the most important attacker profiles as aligned with organizational

risk for your scenarios?
<--- Score

76. Does an optimal size of resource buffer exist for all projects?
<--- Score

77. What error proofing will be done to address some of the discrepancies observed in the 'as is' process?
<--- Score

78. How will the manager validate model results?
<--- Score

79. Describe the design of the pilot and what tests were conducted, if any?
<--- Score

80. Do you need to change it in terms of development?
<--- Score

81. How is knowledge sharing about risk management improved?
<--- Score

82. Risk Identification: What are the possible risk events your organization faces in relation to Movie and Video Production?
<--- Score

83. Have you decided on an overall model and approach to your strategy activity?
<--- Score

84. Does senior management understand the

purpose of models, models limitations, and how models work?
<--- Score

85. What does the 'should be' process map/design look like?
<--- Score

86. How could the service model be improved and strengthened?
<--- Score

87. How do you decide if a set of tests are adequate?
<--- Score

88. Is your current HCM platform an on premise or cloud solution?
<--- Score

89. How did the team generate the list of possible solutions?
<--- Score

90. What criteria will you use to assess your Movie and Video Production risks?
<--- Score

91. Who are the Movie and Video Production decision makers?
<--- Score

92. What area needs the greatest improvement?
<--- Score

93. How would you improve your outsourcing

model?
<--- Score

94. Why developers cannot embed privacy into software systems?
<--- Score

95. How do you decide how much to remunerate an employee?
<--- Score

96. What triggered the decision to innovate your existing business model?
<--- Score

97. What is the overall development timeline?
<--- Score

98. Why has there been developed so many modelling languages?
<--- Score

99. What are the Movie and Video Production security risks?
<--- Score

100. What communications are necessary to support the implementation of the solution?
<--- Score

101. Is the implementation plan designed?
<--- Score

102. Can platforms be a source of new product innovations or product improvements?
<--- Score

103. What are different software development model?
<--- Score

104. Are the risks fully understood, reasonable and manageable?
<--- Score

105. Is the measure of success for Movie and Video Production understandable to a variety of people?
<--- Score

106. Is the model optimum, can it be improved further, is it stuck in local minima?
<--- Score

107. What are your views on the appropriateness of the independence risk model?
<--- Score

108. How well do you design, develop, deliver, innovate and manage?
<--- Score

109. Can knowing something about your organization or individual provide a solution?
<--- Score

110. Is Movie and Video Production documentation maintained?
<--- Score

111. Can you integrate quality management and risk management?
<--- Score

112. Is component/service available for evaluation?
<--- Score

113. Is there a cost/benefit analysis of optimal solution(s)?
<--- Score

114. How can agile development be supported with a matching pricing model and contracts?
<--- Score

115. How are conceptual models used in industrial software development?
<--- Score

116. What is Movie and Video Production risk?
<--- Score

117. Why do you need to improve the system quality?
<--- Score

118. What department head has signed off on the largest business risk?
<--- Score

119. How does your organization evaluate strategic Movie and Video Production success?
<--- Score

120. What is the implementation plan?
<--- Score

121. Were any criteria developed to assist the team in

testing and evaluating potential solutions?
<--- Score

122. Are possible solutions generated and tested?
<--- Score

Add up total points for this section:
_____ = Total points for this section

Divided by: ______ (number of statements answered) = ______ Average score for this section

Transfer your score to the Movie and Video Production Index at the beginning of the Self-Assessment.

CRITERION #6: CONTROL:

INTENT: Implement the practical solution. Maintain the performance and correct possible complications.

In my belief, the answer to this question is clearly defined:

5 Strongly Agree

4 Agree

3 Neutral

2 Disagree

1 Strongly Disagree

1. What do you measure to verify effectiveness gains?
<--- Score

2. How do you check your model, and verify the entered steps for the plan?
<--- Score

3. What models and criteria are available for succession planning?

<--- Score

4. How many system builds are planned?
<--- Score

5. Has the improved process and its steps been standardized?
<--- Score

6. Do you filter the requirements based on frameworks, standards, or risk?
<--- Score

7. How much of the underlying system is available through reflection?
<--- Score

8. What are you doing to protect ourselves against the threats?
<--- Score

9. What do your reports reflect?
<--- Score

10. Do you currently use or plan to use any technologies in payroll?
<--- Score

11. Is a response plan in place for when the input, process, or output measures indicate an 'out-of-control' condition?
<--- Score

12. Are there appropriate controls for protecting sensitive customer information?
<--- Score

13. Are industry standards or a specific method/ model followed for software development?
<--- Score

14. What resources, tools and models should you put in place to monitor value creation?
<--- Score

15. Do you have plans to shift to a multi functional model?
<--- Score

16. How will the day-to-day responsibilities for monitoring and continual improvement be transferred from the improvement team to the process owner?
<--- Score

17. Does a troubleshooting guide exist or is it needed?
<--- Score

18. What should the next improvement project be that is related to Movie and Video Production?
<--- Score

19. How does your current support model scale with your business?
<--- Score

20. How to explicitly model the uncertainty and risk created by climate change in power system planning?
<--- Score

21. How will the process owner and team be able to

hold the gains?
<--- Score

22. How will input, process, and output variables be checked to detect for sub-optimal conditions?
<--- Score

23. Are suggested corrective/restorative actions indicated on the response plan for known causes to problems that might surface?
<--- Score

24. How do you begin to plan your transition to a subscription based infrastructure model?
<--- Score

25. Is the value of the work accomplished tracked and monitored?
<--- Score

26. Does your organization use established data models or standards for collecting asset data?
<--- Score

27. What is the control/monitoring plan?
<--- Score

28. You may have created your quality measures at a time when you lacked resources, technology wasn't up to the required standard, or low service levels were the industry norm. Have those circumstances changed?
<--- Score

29. How much does the incremental learning affect the workload models?

<--- Score

30. Is new knowledge gained imbedded in the response plan?
<--- Score

31. How will new or emerging customer needs/requirements be checked/communicated to orient the process toward meeting the new specifications and continually reducing variation?
<--- Score

32. Do you plan to shift to a multi functional model?
<--- Score

33. Does the response plan contain a definite closed loop continual improvement scheme (e.g., plan-do-check-act)?
<--- Score

34. What are the main implications of outsourcing on the supply chain operations planning models?
<--- Score

35. What is the recommended frequency of auditing?
<--- Score

36. Who will be in control?
<--- Score

37. Are there documented procedures?
<--- Score

38. Are documented procedures clear and easy to follow for the operators?

<--- Score

39. Are new process steps, standards, and documentation ingrained into normal operations?
<--- Score

40. How long is the project planned to take?
<--- Score

41. Is it a place that models planning behavior?
<--- Score

42. What is your reflection on the presented model?
<--- Score

43. Have new or revised work instructions resulted?
<--- Score

44. What quality tools were useful in the control phase?
<--- Score

45. Why have you opted against using a multi functional model?
<--- Score

46. Is the form of BCM implemented in your organization modeled after any relevant standard related to BCM?
<--- Score

47. Does the Movie and Video Production performance meet the customer's requirements?
<--- Score

48. Does the business need to create/update its business continuity plan?
<--- Score

49. Do you have plans to shift to a multifunctional model?
<--- Score

50. How do you monitor usage and cost?
<--- Score

51. When the notation or language has been learned, can the rest be inferred?
<--- Score

52. Does the standard form contract contain KPIs?
<--- Score

53. Is there documentation that will support the successful operation of the improvement?
<--- Score

54. Is a response plan established and deployed?
<--- Score

55. How will report readings be checked to effectively monitor performance?
<--- Score

56. Is there a transfer of ownership and knowledge to process owner and process team tasked with the responsibilities.
<--- Score

57. Do you plan to shift to a multifunctional model?

<--- Score

58. Are you using a standardized risk management process?
<--- Score

59. What other systems, operations, processes, and infrastructures (hiring practices, staffing, training, incentives/rewards, metrics/dashboards/scorecards, etc.) need updates, additions, changes, or deletions in order to facilitate knowledge transfer and improvements?
<--- Score

60. What is business strategy & planning consulting?
<--- Score

61. What are the advantages of using a spreadsheet package to create and solve linear programming models?
<--- Score

62. What is the value of models in marketing planning?
<--- Score

63. How might the group capture best practices and lessons learned so as to leverage improvements?
<--- Score

64. What is your plan to assess your security risks?
<--- Score

65. Is there a process to review all mitigations against business priorities?

<--- Score

66. What other areas of the group might benefit from the Movie and Video Production team's improvements, knowledge, and learning?
<--- Score

67. Are design standards optimized to fulfil service need at lowest cost?
<--- Score

68. Does job training on the documented procedures need to be part of the process team's education and training?
<--- Score

69. Which planning models can be used to support the learning and innovation processes that occur in connection with the planning, implementation and use of information systems?
<--- Score

70. How should the data outputs of machine learning models be used, stored, and reused?
<--- Score

71. How long is the first development cycle planned to take?
<--- Score

72. What scenario planning or other models are used in setting the risk appetite and tolerances?
<--- Score

73. How to design and plan sustainable supply chains through optimization models?

<--- Score

74. Is knowledge gained on process shared and institutionalized?
<--- Score

75. What are the critical parameters to watch?
<--- Score

76. How will the process owner verify improvement in present and future sigma levels, process capabilities?
<--- Score

77. How do controls support value?
<--- Score

78. What is the service model that you need to plan for?
<--- Score

79. Is there a documented and implemented monitoring plan?
<--- Score

80. Are operating procedures consistent?
<--- Score

81. How many design reviews are planned?
<--- Score

82. Will any special training be provided for results interpretation?
<--- Score

83. Are all the product processes covered by the plan?

<--- Score

84. What key inputs and outputs are being measured on an ongoing basis?
<--- Score

85. What data standards are already in place at your organization?
<--- Score

86. Is reporting being used or needed?
<--- Score

87. Is there a recommended audit plan for routine surveillance inspections of Movie and Video Production's gains?
<--- Score

88. How are planning, prioritization, funding and oversight of data center services accomplished?
<--- Score

89. How does decentralized control work in industry wide blockchain systems?
<--- Score

90. Do the viable solutions scale to future needs?
<--- Score

91. What is the standards you use to benchmark your IT Security model?
<--- Score

92. What are the shortcomings of traditional project management planning techniques?
<--- Score

93. Who is the Movie and Video Production process owner?
<--- Score

94. How could a deep learning model be designed to predict back orders?
<--- Score

95. Is the spreadsheet used as a model or for modeling?
<--- Score

96. What changes can large scale language models bring?
<--- Score

97. Does the business case reflect a positive benefit?
<--- Score

98. Is there a standardized process?
<--- Score

99. Is there a way to build forecasting scenarios that look at a conservative, moderate, and potentially harsh economic model planning?
<--- Score

100. Is there a control plan in place for sustaining improvements (short and long-term)?
<--- Score

Add up total points for this section:
_____ = Total points for this section

Divided by: ______ (number of statements answered) = ______ Average score for this section

Transfer your score to the Movie and Video Production Index at the beginning of the Self-Assessment.

CRITERION #7: SUSTAIN:

INTENT: Retain the benefits.

In my belief, the answer to this question is clearly defined:

5 Strongly Agree

4 Agree

3 Neutral

2 Disagree

1 Strongly Disagree

1. Where do your models stand with respect to business concerns?
<--- Score

2. Is that still true, or have things changed over the years?
<--- Score

3. Are there user accounts and passwords to protect?
<--- Score

4. Does a physical system have to exist before a digital twin is created?
<--- Score

5. What is a parallel computing system?
<--- Score

6. Which architecture should be used to model the mux device?
<--- Score

7. How can CMMi increase the likelihood that models succeed?
<--- Score

8. What is capability maturity model or project management maturity model?
<--- Score

9. How are vendors notified of system troubles?
<--- Score

10. What are the non traditional talent models within shared services?
<--- Score

11. Which organizational model BEST supports a DevOps culture?
<--- Score

12. What innovation models, if any, have you used in structuring your organization?
<--- Score

13. What distinguishes complex adaptive systems

from other kinds of systems?
<--- Score

14. How will your business model change?
<--- Score

15. What is the difference between a security and privacy threat model?
<--- Score

16. How satisfied are the stakeholders?
<--- Score

17. What are the implications of service orientation for enterprise architecture?
<--- Score

18. What different kinds of service models are there in the reverse logistics field?
<--- Score

19. Why do other organizations suffer with old systems?
<--- Score

20. How flexible are the services and pricing models?
<--- Score

21. Does the model consciously work towards and actually accomplish reduction of pull out programs?
<--- Score

22. Are the change model, IT strategies and KPIs reviewed on a regular basis?

<--- Score

23. What was your first reaction on the innovation of the existing business model?
<--- Score

24. Are incident and service reports maintained at a central site?
<--- Score

25. Should a full model object be returned?
<--- Score

26. How do you determine the quality of the staff assigned to your account?
<--- Score

27. What are the criteria in the selection of a procurement operating model?
<--- Score

28. What is your ownership model going to look like in the future?
<--- Score

29. What are the rules necessary to achieve the business goals?
<--- Score

30. Does digital business model innovation follow a stepwise approach?
<--- Score

31. Are you integrating with a SIEM that extracts security incidents and attacks based on best practices?

<--- Score

32. How does your organization typically form teams?
<--- Score

33. How should high tech established organizations innovate the existing software business model?
<--- Score

34. What operating, and delivery models will be in place throughout integration and how are customers expected to react?
<--- Score

35. How does or would blockchain fit into your organizations business model and strategy?
<--- Score

36. What challenges are related to the initiation of a circular business model?
<--- Score

37. What is the Direct Contracting Model?
<--- Score

38. Should CMMi review and expand or build on past models that show promise?
<--- Score

39. Is the service or service line low to medium value add?
<--- Score

40. How to provide a generic model capable of

representing pragmatic interoperability among systems?
<--- Score

41. Is the threat to a client or a server?
<--- Score

42. What is the enterprise pricing model?
<--- Score

43. What elements of the shared responsibility model will you manage?
<--- Score

44. What is communications and change management consulting?
<--- Score

45. Why is security engineering important?
<--- Score

46. Does the objectives of the model are achieved by the conceptual model?
<--- Score

47. What elements of the models assisted staff and organizations?
<--- Score

48. Is your organization expecting to change its business model or the products or services it offers?
<--- Score

49. How mature is the KPI regime for investment in cybersecurity?

<--- Score

50. What model or steps was used to integrate management systems?
<--- Score

51. What could disrupt your business model or harm your organizations earnings potential?
<--- Score

52. How do shared services differ from other forms of streamlining?
<--- Score

53. Does the current model support the overall organizational strategy?
<--- Score

54. What do you see as the main barriers to changing your organizations business model?
<--- Score

55. How can system integration be enhanced with information models?
<--- Score

56. How could the business model be designed to support circularity and limit leakage to grey market?
<--- Score

57. What are the modeling elements used to capture privacy concepts and the relationships?
<--- Score

58. What do software architects really do?

<--- Score

59. What is your organizations mission?
<--- Score

60. Should you record that as a tampering threat or a spoofing threat?
<--- Score

61. Does the service utilise the asset fully?
<--- Score

62. Does your siem have detection models?
<--- Score

63. How valuable are out of box correlation rules and detection models?
<--- Score

64. What would you differently next time?
<--- Score

65. Does the threat model adhere to internal and external policies?
<--- Score

66. Is the om flexible and adaptable to business model changes given the market conditions?
<--- Score

67. How healthy are your customer experiences?
<--- Score

68. What lines of business are supported?
<--- Score

69. Will organization meetings go online?
<--- Score

70. What is the role of the circular business model in companies?
<--- Score

71. Who can give you a straightforward pricing model to the cloud?
<--- Score

72. Is it clear what projects were used to construct each model?
<--- Score

73. How is the BCM communicated in your organization?
<--- Score

74. What change must be effected at the administrative and management levels to support success of the redesigned business model?
<--- Score

75. What are the main directions of using rewriting rules systems?
<--- Score

76. Which qualitative differences of the service tailored workload models exist?
<--- Score

77. Is the service or service line high value add?
<--- Score

78. What percentage of business services are

governed properly within the project?
<--- Score

79. How do you help system engineers to design more efficiently and rationally?
<--- Score

80. What is a team model of service delivery?
<--- Score

81. Is there anything else that you think should be changed in the model?
<--- Score

82. What have been the benefits of moving to a multi functional model?
<--- Score

83. What level of maintenance spares are available?
<--- Score

84. When, within a software lifecycle, do you conduct threat modeling?
<--- Score

85. Is the model targeted at a specific technology?
<--- Score

86. What elements of the service delivery models did managers think made a difference?
<--- Score

87. Is the threat model regularly updated through feedback during the value streams?
<--- Score

88. What is your organizations shared services approach?
<--- Score

89. Can an existing investment be leveraged for the new organization?
<--- Score

90. How will translated materials be embedded in the program and model structure?
<--- Score

91. What is causing manufacturers to rethink the service business models regarding remote assets and equipment?
<--- Score

92. What policies and procedures are published for services?
<--- Score

93. What benefits did the BCM have in the past?
<--- Score

94. Is your program logic model accurate to what your program actually works toward?
<--- Score

95. Which organizational model will help you achieve that value?
<--- Score

96. Which cloud service or deployment model is the most appropriate for your organization?
<--- Score

97. What is pulse secures go to market model?
<--- Score

98. What sort of pricing models have you validated?
<--- Score

99. What effect on the exponential smoothing model will increasing the smoothing constant have?
<--- Score

100. Is the component/service specification provided?
<--- Score

101. What are your business reasons for moving to a shared service delivery model?
<--- Score

102. Which features should an ideal tool have to efficiently support program comprehension?
<--- Score

103. How do other organizations survive over the long term?
<--- Score

104. Do your operational staffs have knowledge on Cybersecurity?
<--- Score

105. What are the batch sizes of the models?
<--- Score

106. What will be the pace of roll out of % the new payment model throughout your organization?
<--- Score

107. Is the bcm sufficiently communicated in the relevant departments, it and business?
<--- Score

108. Which methodology was used to create the model?
<--- Score

109. Is there security legislation you must comply with?
<--- Score

110. What service model of cloud computing are you using?
<--- Score

111. Does your organizational model notice?
<--- Score

112. How do you access your organization of the whole system at any particular point of its evolution?
<--- Score

113. Do you have clear relationships across the stack, between key assets in the inventory?
<--- Score

114. Is the knowledge accessible to others for determining additional mitigations?
<--- Score

115. How do you know when to make a change to the model?
<--- Score

116. Is the business model very centralized?
<--- Score

117. How will shared services adapt to the new operating model?
<--- Score

118. Are the security mechanisms working properly?
<--- Score

119. What types of business models seem to work within the market?
<--- Score

120. Why are you looking to change your current support model?
<--- Score

121. How are new team members brought up to speed on the architecture?
<--- Score

122. What are the formal languages and methods of systems engineering?
<--- Score

123. What is the purpose of your organization?
<--- Score

124. Are there other interorganization projects that would be a good model to use with

sustainable procurement?
<--- Score

125. Does the logical model provide enough components for cloud platform?
<--- Score

126. What is the difference between your strategy, operating model, and governance?
<--- Score

127. What security advantage does firmware have over software?
<--- Score

128. How do you match your high performance, highly isolated network model?
<--- Score

129. What is the model for a servant leader?
<--- Score

130. Does your organization have the internal capacity to implement a shared service model?
<--- Score

131. Are web services fundamentally predicated on the web?
<--- Score

132. What are some advantages and disadvantages of a free and open source software model?
<--- Score

133. What is a cloud operating model and how is

different from any other operating model that IT has delivered in the past?
<--- Score

134. What security approach/model do you follow for your Power BI projects?
<--- Score

135. Which model represents the best fit with your current service delivery system and environment?
<--- Score

136. Are procurement shared services nearing the best by date?
<--- Score

137. What do it managers have to do for the services to gain wide acceptance?
<--- Score

138. What are the characteristics of security threat models?
<--- Score

139. What is the difference between statistical models and market based models?
<--- Score

140. What is the role of a systems architect in systems engineering?
<--- Score

141. Do you have any open security bugs?
<--- Score

142. What human resources are available to work

on the projects or as subject matter experts?
<--- Score

143. Does the component respond to messages as specified by changes in what it will respond to?
<--- Score

144. What business models have been used in similar ventures?
<--- Score

145. Is it just the service instances that have identity, or also the model instances?
<--- Score

146. What is organizations strategy regarding mergers and acquisitions?
<--- Score

147. What is the updated model timeline?
<--- Score

148. What percentage of services are created as IT services?
<--- Score

149. Does the conceptual model provide enough components for DevOps?
<--- Score

150. What is virtual service delivery?
<--- Score

151. Is there privacy legislation you must comply with?
<--- Score

152. What rules should be used to generate a relational model?
<--- Score

153. What are the goals of software verification?
<--- Score

154. What service model of cloud computing are you providing?
<--- Score

155. Have you made any significant changes to your business model strategy since the last shocks?
<--- Score

156. What makes a sustainable business model successful?
<--- Score

157. What benefits will the BCM have in the future?
<--- Score

158. What service delivery model do you primarily follow for payroll?
<--- Score

159. Do you stick to one model at a time?
<--- Score

160. Is it possible to add a default scenario to an existing model or program and generate automatically the tolerant model or program?
<--- Score

161. What feature enables code to be executed without the usual security checks?
<--- Score

162. Can a cloud providers security be tuned to every business model and workflow of all its customers?
<--- Score

163. How are users trouble calls administered?
<--- Score

164. How is system spare capacity tracked?
<--- Score

165. What are the key tasks within the new service delivery model?
<--- Score

166. What metrics or KPIs will be used to confirm that the objective has been met?
<--- Score

167. How will the team assess quality as the increment is modeled, constructed, and deployed?
<--- Score

168. Will cloud computing lead you to thin client model?
<--- Score

169. Where is there flexibility to adapt existing services and where should model and program elements remain the same?
<--- Score

170. What are the potential business models for the different shared services structural types?
<--- Score

171. What is the procedure for requests for new services and equipment?
<--- Score

172. How will configuration management of the model be maintained?
<--- Score

173. Is the service or service line transactional or routine in nature?
<--- Score

174. How will you launch quality product fast onto the market on new devices, stealing market share?
<--- Score

175. Does correctional program quality really matter?
<--- Score

176. What makes the business model successful?
<--- Score

177. What are the disadvantages of the client/ server model?
<--- Score

178. What are the advantages of client/server model?
<--- Score

179. How are other organizations designing

themselves for digitally enabled business model innovation?
<--- Score

180. What are the consequences of implementing the integrated model in your organization?
<--- Score

181. Will your system resist attackers who have broken in and scraped the account?
<--- Score

182. What are the important subsystems?
<--- Score

183. What is how the hybrid paperless model works?
<--- Score

184. Does emissions modelling capture climate change?
<--- Score

185. Can the strengths of the various models be represented in a single comprehensive IT value model?
<--- Score

186. How many functions are performed and what is the preferred governance model?
<--- Score

187. Is your organization ready for the new consumption and transaction models that are enabled by cloud?
<--- Score

188. What statistical models have been formulated?
<--- Score

189. Do you provide any predictive modeling tools for the client or consultants use?
<--- Score

190. How do key elements of the business work together to realize strategy and the business models?
<--- Score

191. What business change does the enterprise expect from SOA?
<--- Score

192. What forms should runtime models take?
<--- Score

193. Is the service or service line non transactional and non routine in nature?
<--- Score

194. What are your organizations values?
<--- Score

195. What experience do you have in managing a system in a Maintenance and Operations type model?
<--- Score

196. Who are you currently working with?
<--- Score

197. Are you driving the transaction economic modeling and financial due diligence?
<--- Score

198. What model has been implemented in your organization to manage crisis, and under what scenarios?
<--- Score

199. Which cloud model should you use?
<--- Score

200. What is the most important criterion when your organization chooses a project selection model?
<--- Score

201. What are the key implications to your GRC models?
<--- Score

202. Will the customer accept your system?
<--- Score

203. How do you gain assurance that software is secure enough for its intended use?
<--- Score

204. What are the factors that affect supply chain management?
<--- Score

205. Who could benefit from transforming the service delivery model?
<--- Score

206. What is model lifecycle management?
<--- Score

207. Why adopt the Quality CoE model?
<--- Score

208. Who will serve on the board of directors of the combined organization?
<--- Score

209. Do the mac addresses of the source and destination align with the ip addresses?
<--- Score

210. What is threat modeling and why it is important?
<--- Score

211. What kind of information elements do model stores provide?
<--- Score

212. Does the logical model provide enough components for the cloud platform?
<--- Score

213. How large of a model does your tool handle?
<--- Score

214. What elements should be considered when selecting a team structure and staffing model?
<--- Score

215. Are internal customers allowed to buy IT services from external providers?
<--- Score

216. Where are all your security components?
<--- Score

217. What are the most important means for achieving syntactic quality?
<--- Score

218. What percentage of services are going to be realized through access services?
<--- Score

219. Can anyone replace the manager at any time?
<--- Score

220. What is the communitys governance model?
<--- Score

221. How do services influence the asset portfolio?
<--- Score

222. Do you have only minutes to build an enterprise grade cloud infrastructure?
<--- Score

223. What types of resourcing supply chain models are used and why?
<--- Score

224. How to design for a UX journey and orchestrate the touchpoints of the experiences?
<--- Score

225. Should dialogue models retrieve over more than just factual knowledge?
<--- Score

226. Are there multiple applications for the same capability?
<--- Score

227. What percentage of services are considered adaptable?
<--- Score

228. How can be sure accuracy of performance before implementation of changes in real environment?
<--- Score

229. Do you have your organization model applicable across geographies?
<--- Score

230. Why have digital service teams been created in the first place?
<--- Score

231. Is there anything more on the model?
<--- Score

232. How can engineers reduce the design time of a desired mission and system?
<--- Score

233. What makes the service concept so appealing for enterprise architecture practice?
<--- Score

234. Who are the intended users of the Strategic Workforce Model?
<--- Score

235. How to make sure of the performance before implementation and integration?
<--- Score

236. How is security engineering practiced within your organization?
<--- Score

237. What are your views on alternative price models for SaaS based systems?
<--- Score

238. Does the logical model provide enough components for DevOps?
<--- Score

239. Does the physical model provide enough features for cloud?
<--- Score

240. What types of organizations can apply for the Direct Contracting model?
<--- Score

241. Have you considered the significance of individual metrics to your business model?
<--- Score

242. What is the analogy to information systems architecture and enterprise architecture?
<--- Score

243. How do you help system engineers to design more rationally and efficiently?
<--- Score

244. Are you currently an active software architect?
<--- Score

245. Does your organization fit the service delivery model?
<--- Score

246. Which ways of financing and business models are there?
<--- Score

247. Is iaas the right sourcing model for your business?
<--- Score

248. How is the time dimension specified in the model?
<--- Score

249. What percentage of services are going to be realized through direct exposure?
<--- Score

250. What was the reasons to introduce a 3D system or why would it be necessary?
<--- Score

251. What is the final step in authorizing a system for use in an environment?
<--- Score

252. Do the employees who are responsible for handling taxable accounts have the skills and capabilities to ensure the compliance of invoice

issuance?
<--- Score

253. What is lifecycle modeling language?
<--- Score

254. What are the important elements from the model?
<--- Score

255. What software reuse benefits have been transferred to the industry?
<--- Score

256. How might you use a model of a system that already exists?
<--- Score

257. Will one model work for all services?
<--- Score

258. What modeling languages capture privacy concepts?
<--- Score

259. Do you have the right accountability model in place for cybersecurity?
<--- Score

260. Which approach to organization design will enable greater speed and responsiveness?
<--- Score

261. What were the key challenges to get the code running?
<--- Score

262. Do you know your business model?
<--- Score

263. Which are the most common challenges when initiating and implementing a circular business model?
<--- Score

264. Do you have the right business model to continually achieve better levels of performance?
<--- Score

265. What is the effect of different models of pay for performance schemes?
<--- Score

266. Which quality management system model?
<--- Score

267. What challenges are associated with each supply chain model?
<--- Score

268. Is securing everything by design the best way to go about it?
<--- Score

269. Does the business model make sense?
<--- Score

270. What are the drawbacks of spiral model?
<--- Score

271. What services utilise your current asset portfolio?

<--- Score

272. What business models are you considering?
<--- Score

273. How does the competitors business model look like?
<--- Score

274. What are the privacy concepts captured by modeling languages?
<--- Score

275. How do you support the evolution of a system while maintaining its integrity?
<--- Score

276. Does the system maintain an audit trail of transactions reported?
<--- Score

277. How does business mashups differ from enterprise portals?
<--- Score

278. Who will benefit from your work here?
<--- Score

279. Are climate adaptation and mitigation strategic goals to your organization?
<--- Score

280. What are the general principles applicable to systems?
<--- Score

281. Do you have internal knowledge bases to construct your threat model?
<--- Score

282. Does model based systems engineering approach provide real program savings?
<--- Score

283. What do security engineering activities encompass?
<--- Score

284. What are changes to the service delivery model?
<--- Score

285. Are models tailored for specific applications and informed by business uses?
<--- Score

286. Are you complying with existing security policies?
<--- Score

287. How do you know the model can work well on the unexpected runtime input/sample?
<--- Score

288. How to introduce changes into the system while preserving its integrity?
<--- Score

289. Why is systems engineering important?
<--- Score

290. How should advisors leverage the continuum

of business models?
<--- Score

291. Will redefining an asset make it more attractive to other/new services?
<--- Score

292. What is specific about each system?
<--- Score

293. How to keep track of the operations performed for evolving the system?
<--- Score

294. Will the asset be funded by the service?
<--- Score

295. How can the enterprise conform to the specification of the rule?
<--- Score

296. What is the best language for modeling system architecture?
<--- Score

297. How shall scalability be specified and tested?
<--- Score

298. How do you create the funding source and governance models?
<--- Score

299. When is security of a system most effective and economical?
<--- Score

300. Does the vendor support a content delivery network model?
<--- Score

301. Why should auditors know about SDLC models?
<--- Score

302. What are the nontraditional talent models within shared services?
<--- Score

303. Does the physical model provide enough features for the cloud?
<--- Score

304. Do some business models perform better than others?
<--- Score

305. Where do you find a pricing model that actually makes sense?
<--- Score

306. Are you using some type of industry knowledge base as a reference?
<--- Score

307. Do all classify the instances in the same way at all times?
<--- Score

308. What tool support is used for the activities shown in the model?
<--- Score

309. Is your organization committed to working with other partners in delivering the shared services?
<--- Score

310. Should the estimated variance covariance be included in the fitted model object?
<--- Score

311. How is performance affected through variations within the system?
<--- Score

312. Does the conceptual model provide enough components for the cloud?
<--- Score

313. What are the strengths and weaknesses of the current service delivery model?
<--- Score

314. What aspects of a service should be specified?
<--- Score

315. How representative for future workload scenarios are workload models with forecasted intensities?
<--- Score

316. Is there any implied scenario in the system architecture model?
<--- Score

317. How should management of security functions be split?
<--- Score

318. What are the advantages of mixed model sequencing?
<--- Score

319. How valuable are the out of the box detection models?
<--- Score

320. Why are other organizations trapped?
<--- Score

321. Will your system use only information that only you and your customer should know?
<--- Score

322. What vulnerabilities can the threat exploits?
<--- Score

323. What is a deterministic transition system?
<--- Score

324. Does the physical model provide enough features for IoT apps deployment?
<--- Score

325. Does internal audit have the appropriate skills and adequate stature in your organization?
<--- Score

326. Which model deals only with confidentiality?
<--- Score

327. What is the sequence in which the models will be introduced onto the line?
<--- Score

328. Should you test the model or the production code?
<--- Score

329. How many gigabit ethernet interfaces does the switch have?
<--- Score

330. What is your AI score for doing breakout business model innovation?
<--- Score

331. Should businesses be thinking about decentralized business models as well?
<--- Score

332. How do assets influence the services portfolio?
<--- Score

333. Is the client tech savvy enough to fit your business model?
<--- Score

334. Can maturity models support cybersecurity?
<--- Score

335. Where is threat modeling headed?
<--- Score

336. Which are the probabilities of system failure?
<--- Score

337. What should your cloud operating model look like?

<--- Score

338. How is the information for each metric interpreted and managed?
<--- Score

339. Does the research model hold under various products and services?
<--- Score

340. Do you associate multiple threat models for your system?
<--- Score

341. Are you considering a model to do real time budget forecasting versus the traditional annual budget approach?
<--- Score

342. Where and how can information models be used to support system integration?
<--- Score

343. What information would be relevant for the views?
<--- Score

344. Which of your sellers get it with regard to the new consumption models?
<--- Score

345. What is the market size and estimate of market share?
<--- Score

346. What are the formal languages of systems

engineering?
<--- Score

347. Does the customer have your organization partner channel model?
<--- Score

348. What are fault models for software?
<--- Score

349. Does the logical model provide enough components for IoT apps deployment?
<--- Score

350. Which organizational performance models are available in literature?
<--- Score

351. Which geographic models is used?
<--- Score

352. Are there corporate security policies that must be adhered to?
<--- Score

353. What do the current business models look like for each business model?
<--- Score

354. What is capital projects & infrastructure consulting?
<--- Score

355. What types of partnership models are used by independent software vendors in software sales?
<--- Score

356. What type of voice system do you have, hardware vendor make and model?
<--- Score

357. What is your organization model?
<--- Score

358. Why is an object included in the structure of collaborating objects?
<--- Score

359. What is the structure of the new organization?
<--- Score

360. Are business models emerging that service providers should consider when looking to manage multiple, complex services?
<--- Score

361. What types of inventory models are applied and what extent?
<--- Score

362. Does the physical model provide enough features for DevOps?
<--- Score

363. Which models should you include in the accuracy chart?
<--- Score

364. What is spiking network modeling?
<--- Score

365. How closely is the system tied to a single

model of work?
<--- Score

366. What are the different types of service delivery?
<--- Score

367. How can well meaning providers and the staff empower consumers?
<--- Score

368. What are the main factors affect the synchronization of supply chain members?
<--- Score

369. How do you ensure your pricing model is profitable?
<--- Score

370. Do you have the right operating model to partner with the business?
<--- Score

371. What sources of information are at your disposal or are available to you?
<--- Score

372. What is the service delivery model?
<--- Score

373. What are the next steps towards actual services?
<--- Score

374. Which is a weakness of the spiral model?
<--- Score

375. How does the extended management model differ from the basic management model?
<--- Score

376. Does the generated code implements the conceptual model?
<--- Score

377. What does it really gain you to deliver technology via an internal services model?
<--- Score

378. What behavior is expected of the systems?
<--- Score

379. How do you build a model that fits an incremental sales approach?
<--- Score

380. How will changes of operator occupations affect system/task performance?
<--- Score

Add up total points for this section:
_____ = Total points for this section

Divided by: ______ (number of statements answered) = ______ Average score for this section

Transfer your score to the Movie and Video Production Index at the beginning of the Self-Assessment.

Movie And Video Production and Managing Projects, Criteria for Project Managers:

1.0 Initiating Process Group: Movie And Video Production

1. In which Movie And Video Production project management process group is the detailed Movie And Video Production project budget created?

2. Although the Movie And Video Production project manager does not directly manage procurement and contracting activities, who does manage procurement and contracting activities in your organization then if not the PM?

3. Contingency planning. if a risk event occurs, what will you do?

4. Does it make any difference if you am successful?

5. Do you understand the quality and control criteria that must be achieved for successful Movie And Video Production project completion?

6. Are the changes in your Movie And Video Production project being formally requested, analyzed, and approved by the appropriate decision makers?

7. At which cmmi level are software processes documented, standardized, and integrated into a standard to-be practiced process for your organization?

8. Are you properly tracking the progress of the Movie And Video Production project and communicating the status to stakeholders?

9. What will you do?

10. Were resources available as planned?

11. How will you know you did it?

12. How do you help others satisfy needs?

13. How will it affect me?

14. What are the tools and techniques to be used in each phase?

15. What will you do to minimize the impact should a risk event occur?

16. Do you know all the stakeholders impacted by the Movie And Video Production project and what needs are?

17. What input will you be required to provide the Movie And Video Production project team?

18. What do they need to know about the Movie And Video Production project?

19. At which stage, in a typical Movie And Video Production project do stake holders have maximum influence?

20. What are the inputs required to produce the deliverables?

1.1 Project Charter: Movie And Video Production

21. Why the improvements?

22. When?

23. Why Outsource?

24. Is it an improvement over existing products?

25. What is the justification?

26. What are the assumptions?

27. What outcome, in measureable terms, are you hoping to accomplish?

28. Why is it important?

29. Pop quiz – which are the same inputs as in the Movie And Video Production project charter?

30. What goes into your Movie And Video Production project Charter?

31. How will you know that a change is an improvement?

32. What barriers do you predict to your success?

33. Customer benefits: what customer requirements does this Movie And Video Production project

address?

34. Customer: who are you doing the Movie And Video Production project for?

35. Who is the Movie And Video Production project Manager?

36. How are Movie And Video Production projects different from operations?

37. Why use a Movie And Video Production project charter?

38. What are the deliverables?

39. How will you learn more about the process or system you are trying to improve?

40. Where does all this information come from?

1.2 Stakeholder Register: Movie And Video Production

41. What & Why?

42. How should employers make voices heard?

43. Is your organization ready for change?

44. What is the power of the stakeholder?

45. What are the major Movie And Video Production project milestones requiring communications or providing communications opportunities?

46. Who is managing stakeholder engagement?

47. What opportunities exist to provide communications?

48. Who are the stakeholders?

49. How big is the gap?

50. How much influence do they have on the Movie And Video Production project?

51. How will reports be created?

52. Who wants to talk about Security?

1.3 Stakeholder Analysis Matrix: Movie And Video Production

53. Alliances: with which other actors is the actor allied, how are they interconnected?

54. How will the stakeholder directly benefit from the Movie And Video Production project and how will this affect the stakeholders motivation?

55. What are the reimbursement requirements?

56. Partnership opportunities/synergies?

57. What tools would help you communicate?

58. Who will be affected by the Movie And Video Production project?

59. Which conditions out of the control of the management are crucial to contribute for the achievement of the development objective?

60. What do your organizations stakeholders do better than anyone else?

61. Who has the power to influence the outcomes of the work?

62. Who is most dependent on the resources at stake?

63. How to involve media?

64. Business and product development?

65. How to measure the achievement of the Development Objective?

66. Who will be responsible for managing the outcome?

67. Sustaining internal capabilities?

68. Who holds positions of responsibility in interested organizations?

69. Who will be affected by the Movie And Video Production project?

70. Management cover, succession?

71. Inoculations or payment to receive them?

72. Are you working on the right risks?

2.0 Planning Process Group: Movie And Video Production

73. What types of differentiated effects are resulting from the Movie And Video Production project and to what extent?

74. Are the necessary foundations in place to ensure the sustainability of the results of the Movie And Video Production project?

75. Explanation: is what the Movie And Video Production project intents to solve a hard question?

76. How well did the chosen processes fit the needs of the Movie And Video Production project?

77. What good practices or successful experiences or transferable examples have been identified?

78. If a task is partitionable, is this a sufficient condition to reduce the Movie And Video Production project duration?

79. Does it make any difference if you are successful?

80. Mitigate. what will you do to minimize the impact should a risk event occur?

81. To what extent has a PMO contributed to raising the quality of the design of the Movie And Video Production project?

82. How should needs be met?

83. You did your readings, yes?

84. Is the Movie And Video Production project making progress in helping to achieve the set results?

85. Why is it important to determine activity sequencing on Movie And Video Production projects?

86. If task x starts two days late, what is the effect on the Movie And Video Production project end date?

87. What do they need to know about the Movie And Video Production project?

88. On which process should team members spend the most time?

89. Is the duration of the program sufficient to ensure a cycle that will Movie And Video Production project the sustainability of the interventions?

90. Who are the Movie And Video Production project stakeholders?

2.1 Project Management Plan: Movie And Video Production

91. What went right?

92. Do there need to be organizational changes?

93. Are cost risk analysis methods applied to develop contingencies for the estimated total Movie And Video Production project costs?

94. What data/reports/tools/etc. do your PMs need?

95. Who manages integration?

96. What happened during the process that you found interesting?

97. Who is the sponsor?

98. Are there any Client staffing expectations?

99. How do you organize the costs in the Movie And Video Production project management plan?

100. What if, for example, the positive direction and vision of your organization causes expected trends to change resulting in greater need than expected?

101. Is there anything you would now do differently on your Movie And Video Production project based on past experience?

102. What are the constraints?

103. Who is the Movie And Video Production project Manager?

104. What went wrong?

105. Is the budget realistic?

106. Is mitigation authorized or recommended?

107. What does management expect of PMs?

108. Why Change?

109. What are the training needs?

2.2 Scope Management Plan: Movie And Video Production

110. Has process improvement efforts been completed before requirements efforts begin?

111. Have the key functions and capabilities been defined and assigned to each release or iteration?

112. Is stakeholder involvement adequate?

113. Have activity relationships and interdependencies within tasks been adequately identified?

114. What is the need the Movie And Video Production project will address?

115. Has the Movie And Video Production project scope been baselined?

116. Are post milestone Movie And Video Production project reviews (PMPR) conducted with your organization at least once a year?

117. Personnel with expertise?

118. Are trade-offs between accepting the risk and mitigating the risk identified?

119. Are estimating assumptions and constraints captured?

120. What are the acceptance criteria (process and criteria to be met for key stakeholder acceptance) and who is authorized to sign off?

121. Have all documents been archived in a Movie And Video Production project repository for each release?

122. Do you have the reasons why the changes to your organizational systems and capabilities are required?

123. Have all involved Movie And Video Production project stakeholders and work groups committed to the Movie And Video Production project?

124. Are all resource assumptions documented?

125. Is there an on-going process in place to monitor Movie And Video Production project risks?

126. Has the schedule been baselined?

127. Were Movie And Video Production project team members involved in the development of activity & task decomposition?

128. Are the Movie And Video Production project team members located locally to the users/ stakeholders?

129. What does the critical path really mean?

2.3 Requirements Management Plan: Movie And Video Production

130. What performance metrics will be used?

131. How do you know that you have done this right?

132. How detailed should the Movie And Video Production project get?

133. Should you include sub-activities?

134. Is there formal agreement on who has authority to request a change in requirements?

135. Who will approve the requirements (and if multiple approvers, in what order)?

136. Who will perform the analysis?

137. Does the Movie And Video Production project have a Change Control process?

138. Will you have access to stakeholders when you need them?

139. Will the Movie And Video Production project requirements become approved in writing?

140. Which hardware or software, related to, or as outcome of the Movie And Video Production project is new to your organization?

141. Is the system software (non-operating system) new to the IT Movie And Video Production project team?

142. Who has the authority to reject Movie And Video Production project requirements?

143. Do you have an agreed upon process for alerting the Movie And Video Production project Manager if a request for change in requirements leads to a product scope change?

144. Will you use an assessment of the Movie And Video Production project environment as a tool to discover risk to the requirements process?

145. Will you perform a Requirements Risk assessment and develop a plan to deal with risks?

146. To see if a requirement statement is sufficiently well-defined, read it from the developers perspective. Mentally add the phrase, call me when youre done to the end of the requirement and see if that makes you nervous. In other words, would you need additional clarification from the author to understand the requirement well enough to design and implement it?

147. How will the information be distributed?

148. Who is responsible for monitoring and tracking the Movie And Video Production project requirements?

2.4 Requirements Documentation: Movie And Video Production

149. Completeness. are all functions required by the customer included?

150. Are all functions required by the customer included?

151. Basic work/business process; high-level, what is being touched?

152. Has requirements gathering uncovered information that would necessitate changes?

153. How does the proposed Movie And Video Production project contribute to the overall objectives of your organization?

154. What is the risk associated with cost and schedule?

155. How much does requirements engineering cost?

156. How linear / iterative is your Requirements Gathering process (or will it be)?

157. What will be the integration problems?

158. Can the requirement be changed without a large impact on other requirements?

159. Is the requirement realistically testable?

160. What are the potential disadvantages/ advantages?

161. How will they be documented / shared?

162. Does the system provide the functions which best support the customers needs?

163. Is new technology needed?

164. Who is interacting with the system?

165. Where are business rules being captured?

166. Verifiability. can the requirements be checked?

167. Do technical resources exist?

2.5 Requirements Traceability Matrix: Movie And Video Production

168. What are the chronologies, contingencies, consequences, criteria?

169. Will you use a Requirements Traceability Matrix?

170. How will it affect the stakeholders personally in career?

171. Is there a requirements traceability process in place?

172. Why do you manage scope?

173. Do you have a clear understanding of all subcontracts in place?

174. How do you manage scope?

175. What is the WBS?

176. What percentage of Movie And Video Production projects are producing traceability matrices between requirements and other work products?

177. How small is small enough?

178. Describe the process for approving requirements so they can be added to the traceability matrix and Movie And Video Production project work can be performed. Will the Movie And Video Production

project requirements become approved in writing?

179. Why use a WBS?

2.6 Project Scope Statement: Movie And Video Production

180. Is the plan for your organization of the Movie And Video Production project resources adequate?

181. Elements that deal with providing the detail?

182. Is there a Quality Assurance Plan documented and filed?

183. Once its defined, what is the stability of the Movie And Video Production project scope?

184. Any new risks introduced or old risks impacted. Are there issues that could affect the existing requirements for the result, service, or product if the scope changes?

185. Is the plan for Movie And Video Production project resources adequate?

186. Have you been able to thoroughly document the Movie And Video Production projects assumptions and constraints?

187. Is the plan under configuration management?

188. What actions will be taken to mitigate the risk?

189. Are there specific processes you will use to evaluate and approve/reject changes?

190. Elements of scope management that deal with concept development ?

191. Is the quality function identified and assigned?

192. Have the configuration management functions been assigned?

193. Relevant - ask yourself can you get there; why are you doing this Movie And Video Production project?

194. Is the Movie And Video Production project sponsor function identified and defined?

195. How often do you estimate that the scope might change, and why?

196. Did your Movie And Video Production project ask for this?

2.7 Assumption and Constraint Log: Movie And Video Production

197. How are new requirements or changes to requirements identified?

198. When can log be discarded?

199. How can you prevent/fix violations?

200. Can you perform this task or activity in a more effective manner?

201. Does a documented Movie And Video Production project organizational policy & plan (i.e. governance model) exist?

202. Is staff trained on the software technologies that are being used on the Movie And Video Production project?

203. Are there cosmetic errors that hinder readability and comprehension?

204. Do you know what your customers expectations are regarding this process?

205. Have all stakeholders been identified?

206. Contradictory information between different documents?

207. Is the definition of the Movie And Video

Production project scope clear; what needs to be accomplished?

208. Are there processes defining how software will be developed including development methods, overall timeline for development, software product standards, and traceability?

209. Do the requirements meet the standards of correctness, completeness, consistency, accuracy, and readability?

210. Are there ways to reduce the time it takes to get something approved?

211. Model-building: what data-analytic strategies are useful when building proportional-hazards models?

212. What to do at recovery?

213. No superfluous information or marketing narrative?

214. Is this model reasonable?

215. Have Movie And Video Production project management standards and procedures been established and documented?

216. Can the requirements be traced to the appropriate components of the solution, as well as test scripts?

2.8 Work Breakdown Structure: Movie And Video Production

217. How big is a work-package?

218. Do you need another level?

219. Is it a change in scope?

220. What has to be done?

221. What is the probability that the Movie And Video Production project duration will exceed xx weeks?

222. Can you make it?

223. Why is it useful?

224. How far down?

225. When does it have to be done?

226. When do you stop?

227. How will you and your Movie And Video Production project team define the Movie And Video Production projects scope and work breakdown structure?

228. Is it still viable?

229. When would you develop a Work Breakdown Structure?

230. Where does it take place?

231. How many levels?

232. What is the probability of completing the Movie And Video Production project in less that xx days?

233. How much detail?

2.9 WBS Dictionary: Movie And Video Production

234. Software specification, development, integration, and testing, licenses ?

235. The total budget for the contract (including estimates for authorized and unpriced work)?

236. What are you counting on?

237. Does the contractors system include procedures for measuring the performance of critical subcontractors?

238. Are overhead budgets and costs being handled according to the disclosure statement when applicable, or otherwise properly classified (for example, engineering overhead, IR&D)?

239. Authorization to proceed with all authorized work?

240. Can the contractor substantiate work package and planning package budgets?

241. Should you have a test for each code module?

242. Are control accounts opened and closed based on the start and completion of work contained therein?

243. Cwbs elements to be subcontracted, with

identification of subcontractors?

244. Are retroactive changes to budgets for completed work specifically prohibited in an established procedure, and is this procedure adhered to?

245. Are the requirements for all items of overhead established by rational, traceable processes?

246. Are the overhead pools formally and adequately identified?

247. The anticipated business volume?

248. Knowledgeable Movie And Video Production projections of future performance?

249. Are material costs reported within the same period as that in which BCWP is earned for that material?

250. Changes in the overhead pool and/or organization structures?

251. Budgets assigned to control accounts?

252. Are data elements summarized through the functional organizational structure for progressively higher levels of management?

253. Intermediate schedules, as required, which provide a logical sequence from the master schedule to the control account level?

2.10 Schedule Management Plan: Movie And Video Production

254. Pareto diagrams, statistical sampling, flow charting or trend analysis used quality monitoring?

255. Are assumptions being identified, recorded, analyzed, qualified and closed?

256. What threats might prevent you from getting there?

257. Have the key elements of a coherent Movie And Video Production project management strategy been established?

258. What is the difference between % Complete and % work?

259. Define units of measurement for each resource. For example, are you referencing gallons or liters?

260. Are Movie And Video Production project leaders committed to this Movie And Video Production project full time?

261. Are all payments made according to the contract(s)?

262. List all schedule constraints here. Must the Movie And Video Production project be complete by a specified date?

263. Are there checklists created to determine if all quality processes are followed?

264. Can be realistically shortened (the duration of subsequent tasks)?

265. Are written status reports provided on a designated frequent basis?

266. Have reserves been created to address risks?

267. After initial schedule development, will the schedule be reviewed and validated by the Movie And Video Production project team?

268. Why time management?

269. Quality assurance overheads?

270. Are scheduled deliverables actually delivered?

271. What weaknesses do you have?

272. Do all stakeholders know how to access this repository and where to find the Movie And Video Production project documentation?

2.11 Activity List: Movie And Video Production

273. What did not go as well?

274. Are the required resources available or need to be acquired?

275. When will the work be performed?

276. What will be performed?

277. Is there anything planned that does not need to be here?

278. What is the total time required to complete the Movie And Video Production project if no delays occur?

279. How do you determine the late start (LS) for each activity?

280. The wbs is developed as part of a joint planning session. and how do you know that youhave done this right?

281. Where will it be performed?

282. What went well?

283. What is the probability the Movie And Video Production project can be completed in xx weeks?

284. How will it be performed?

285. In what sequence?

286. Who will perform the work?

287. Is infrastructure setup part of your Movie And Video Production project?

288. What are the critical bottleneck activities?

2.12 Activity Attributes: Movie And Video Production

289. What is the general pattern here?

290. Where else does it apply?

291. How else could the items be grouped?

292. Have you identified the Activity Leveling Priority code value on each activity?

293. What conclusions/generalizations can you draw from this?

294. How many days do you need to complete the work scope with a limit of X number of resources?

295. How much activity detail is required?

296. What is missing?

297. Are the required resources available?

298. Time for overtime?

299. Would you consider either of corresponding activities an outlier?

300. What is your organizations history in doing similar activities?

301. Is there a trend during the year?

302. Why?

303. Can you re-assign any activities to another resource to resolve an over-allocation?

304. Do you feel very comfortable with your prediction?

2.13 Milestone List: Movie And Video Production

305. Describe the industry you are in and the market growth opportunities. What is the market for your technology, product or service?

306. Information and research?

307. How soon can the activity finish?

308. What date will the task finish?

309. Describe the concept of the technology, product or service that will be or has been developed. How will it be used?

310. Identify critical paths (one or more) and which activities are on the critical path?

311. Who will manage the Movie And Video Production project on a day-to-day basis?

312. Usps (unique selling points)?

313. Global influences?

314. Reliability of data, plan predictability?

315. Continuity, supply chain robustness?

316. Legislative effects?

317. What background experience, skills, and strengths does the team bring to your organization?

318. Political effects?

319. Loss of key staff?

320. Vital contracts and partners?

321. What would happen if a delivery of material was one week late?

322. Describe your organizations strengths and core competencies. What factors will make your organization succeed?

323. It is to be a narrative text providing the crucial aspects of your Movie And Video Production project proposal answering what, who, how, when and where?

2.14 Network Diagram: Movie And Video Production

324. Where do schedules come from?

325. Review the logical flow of the network diagram. Take a look at which activities you have first and then sequence the activities. Do they make sense?

326. What job or jobs could run concurrently?

327. What is the lowest cost to complete this Movie And Video Production project in xx weeks?

328. Why must you schedule milestones, such as reviews, throughout the Movie And Video Production project?

329. What are the Major Administrative Issues?

330. Which type of network diagram allows you to depict four types of dependencies?

331. What job or jobs follow it?

332. What are the tools?

333. Planning: who, how long, what to do?

334. Are you on time?

335. What job or jobs precede it?

336. If the Movie And Video Production project network diagram cannot change and you have extra personnel resources, what is the BEST thing to do?

337. What controls the start and finish of a job?

338. What can be done concurrently?

339. What activities must follow this activity?

340. Will crashing x weeks return more in benefits than it costs?

341. If x is long, what would be the completion time if you break x into two parallel parts of y weeks and z weeks?

2.15 Activity Resource Requirements: Movie And Video Production

342. Anything else?

343. What are constraints that you might find during the Human Resource Planning process?

344. When does monitoring begin?

345. How many signatures do you require on a check and does this match what is in your policy and procedures?

346. What is the Work Plan Standard?

347. Why do you do that?

348. Other support in specific areas?

349. Organizational Applicability?

350. How do you handle petty cash?

351. How do you manage time?

352. Which logical relationship does the PDM use most often?

353. Are there unresolved issues that need to be addressed?

354. Do you use tools like decomposition and rolling-

wave planning to produce the activity list and other outputs?

2.16 Resource Breakdown Structure: Movie And Video Production

355. The list could probably go on, but, the thing that you would most like to know is, How long & How much?

356. How should the information be delivered?

357. Changes based on input from stakeholders?

358. Is predictive resource analysis being done?

359. What is the number one predictor of a groups productivity?

360. Who needs what information?

361. Who will be used as a Movie And Video Production project team member?

362. How difficult will it be to do specific activities on this Movie And Video Production project?

363. What is the purpose of assigning and documenting responsibility?

364. Why do you do it?

365. When do they need the information?

366. Who is allowed to perform which functions?

367. What can you do to improve productivity?

2.17 Activity Duration Estimates: Movie And Video Production

368. How is the Movie And Video Production project doing?

369. Does a procedure exist to ensure the Movie And Video Production project work is completed in the appropriate sequence and on time?

370. Are actual Movie And Video Production project results compared with planned or expected results to determine the variance?

371. Does a process exist to determine the potential loss or gain if risk events occur?

372. Is training acquired to enhance the skills, knowledge and capabilities of the Movie And Video Production project team?

373. Do they make sense?

374. Based on , if you need to shorten the duration of the Movie And Video Production project, what activity would you try to shorten?

375. Are contractor costs, schedule and technical performance monitored throughout the Movie And Video Production project?

376. If the optimiztic estimate for an activity is 12days, and the pessimistic estimate is 18days, what is the

standard deviation of this activity?

377. Are contingency plans created to prepare for risk events to occur?

378. What functions does this software provide that cannot be done easily using other tools such as a spreadsheet or database?

379. What are the key components of a Movie And Video Production project communications plan?

380. What is the difference between using brainstorming and the Delphi technique for risk identification?

381. Why is there a new or renewed interest in the field of Movie And Video Production project management?

382. Does a process exist to determine which risk events to accept and which events to disregard?

383. What do you think about the WBSs for them?

384. Do procedures exist describing how the Movie And Video Production project scope will be managed?

385. Did anything besides luck make a difference between success and failure?

386. What tasks must follow this task?

387. Movie And Video Production project manager is using weighted average duration estimates to perform schedule network analysis. Which type of

mathematical analysis is being used?

2.18 Duration Estimating Worksheet: Movie And Video Production

388. How should ongoing costs be monitored to try to keep the Movie And Video Production project within budget?

389. What is your role?

390. For other activities, how much delay can be tolerated?

391. Done before proceeding with this activity or what can be done concurrently?

392. When, then?

393. Science = process: remember the scientific method?

394. What is the total time required to complete the Movie And Video Production project if no delays occur?

395. What questions do you have?

396. Will the Movie And Video Production project collaborate with the local community and leverage resources?

397. Value pocket identification & quantification what are value pockets?

398. When do the individual activities need to start and finish?

399. Is this operation cost effective?

400. Does the Movie And Video Production project provide innovative ways for stakeholders to overcome obstacles or deliver better outcomes?

401. What work will be included in the Movie And Video Production project?

402. Can the Movie And Video Production project be constructed as planned?

403. What is next?

404. What utility impacts are there?

2.19 Project Schedule: Movie And Video Production

405. Did the Movie And Video Production project come in on schedule?

406. Meet requirements?

407. Did the final product meet or exceed user expectations?

408. If you can not fix it, how do you do it differently?

409. What is risk management?

410. How can you address that situation?

411. If there are any qualifying green components to this Movie And Video Production project, what portion of the total Movie And Video Production project cost is green?

412. How does a Movie And Video Production project get to be a year late ?

413. How do you know that youhave done this right?

414. Why is this particularly bad?

415. Is there a Schedule Management Plan that establishes the criteria and activities for developing, monitoring and controlling the Movie And Video Production project schedule?

416. Why do you think schedule issues often cause the most conflicts on Movie And Video Production projects?

417. How much slack is available in the Movie And Video Production project?

418. Why do you need schedules?

419. What is risk?

420. Your best shot for providing estimations how complex/how much work does the activity require?

421. How detailed should a Movie And Video Production project get?

422. Why or why not?

423. What is Movie And Video Production project management?

2.20 Cost Management Plan: Movie And Video Production

424. Were Movie And Video Production project team members involved in the development of activity & task decomposition?

425. Have all team members been part of identifying risks?

426. Are metrics used to evaluate and manage Vendors?

427. Have the procedures for identifying budget variances been followed?

428. What is Movie And Video Production project management?

429. What would the life cycle costs be?

430. Are enough systems & user personnel assigned to the Movie And Video Production project?

431. Technical and functional?

432. Has a Movie And Video Production project Communications Plan been developed?

433. Is there a Steering Committee in place?

434. How difficult will it be to do specific tasks on the Movie And Video Production project?

435. Change types and category – What are the types of changes and what are the techniques to report and control changes?

436. Responsibilities – what is the split of responsibilities between the owner and contractors?

437. Does the schedule include Movie And Video Production project management time and change request analysis time?

438. Is it standard practice to formally commit stakeholders to the Movie And Video Production project via agreements?

439. Are parking lot items captured?

440. Has your organization readiness assessment been conducted?

441. Risk Analysis?

442. Is it a Movie And Video Production project?

443. Are schedule deliverables actually delivered?

2.21 Activity Cost Estimates: Movie And Video Production

444. Did the Movie And Video Production project team have the right skills?

445. What is a Movie And Video Production project Management Plan?

446. What is procurement?

447. One way to define activities is to consider how organization employees describe jobs to families and friends. You basically want to know, What do you do?

448. How quickly can the task be done with the skills available?

449. Can you delete activities or make them inactive?

450. Does the estimator estimate by task or by person?

451. What is the activity recast of the budget?

452. How do you treat administrative costs in the activity inventory?

453. Maintenance Reserve?

454. How many activities should you have?

455. Was it performed on time?

456. What were things that you did very well and want to do the same again on the next Movie And Video Production project?

457. The impact and what actions were taken?

458. What is Movie And Video Production project cost management?

459. When do you enter into PPM?

460. Based on your Movie And Video Production project communication management plan, what worked well?

461. Does the activity serve a common type of customer?

462. Will you use any tools, such as Movie And Video Production project management software, to assist in capturing Earned Value metrics?

463. Is costing method consistent with study goals?

2.22 Cost Estimating Worksheet: Movie And Video Production

464. What costs are to be estimated?

465. What can be included?

466. What is the purpose of estimating?

467. Ask: are others positioned to know, are others credible, and will others cooperate?

468. Who is best positioned to know and assist in identifying corresponding factors?

469. What will others want?

470. What is the estimated labor cost today based upon this information?

471. Does the Movie And Video Production project provide innovative ways for stakeholders to overcome obstacles or deliver better outcomes?

472. Identify the timeframe necessary to monitor progress and collect data to determine how the selected measure has changed?

473. What additional Movie And Video Production project(s) could be initiated as a result of this Movie And Video Production project?

474. How will the results be shared and to whom?

475. What info is needed?

476. Is the Movie And Video Production project responsive to community need?

477. Can a trend be established from historical performance data on the selected measure and are the criteria for using trend analysis or forecasting methods met?

478. What happens to any remaining funds not used?

479. Is it feasible to establish a control group arrangement?

480. Will the Movie And Video Production project collaborate with the local community and leverage resources?

2.23 Cost Baseline: Movie And Video Production

481. Have the actual milestone completion dates been compared to the approved schedule?

482. Have the resources used by the Movie And Video Production project been reassigned to other units or Movie And Video Production projects?

483. Verify business objectives. Are others appropriate, and well-articulated?

484. Has the Movie And Video Production projected annual cost to operate and maintain the product(s) or service(s) been approved and funded?

485. If you sold 10x widgets on a day, what would the affect on profits be?

486. What is the most important thing to do next to make your Movie And Video Production project successful?

487. Have the lessons learned been filed with the Movie And Video Production project Management Office?

488. Pcs for your new business. what would the life cycle costs be?

489. Definition of done can be traced back to the definitions of what are you providing to the customer

in terms of deliverables?

490. Review your risk triggers -have your risks changed?

491. Who will use corresponding metrics ?

492. How concrete were original objectives?

493. For what purpose ?

494. Have all approved changes to the cost baseline been identified and impact on the Movie And Video Production project documented?

495. Has the Movie And Video Production project documentation been archived or otherwise disposed as described in the Movie And Video Production project communication plan?

496. How do you manage cost?

497. Does a process exist for establishing a cost baseline to measure Movie And Video Production project performance?

498. Has training and knowledge transfer of the operations organization been completed?

499. How accurate do cost estimates need to be?

2.24 Quality Management Plan: Movie And Video Production

500. Who is approving the QAPP?

501. Are there processes in place to ensure internal consistency between the source code components?

502. Are decisions/actions based on data collected?

503. Checking the completeness and appropriateness of the sampling and testing. Were the right locations/ samples tested for the right parameters?

504. How do you ensure that your sampling methods and procedures meet your data quality objectives?

505. How are your organizations compensation and recognition approaches and the performance management system used to reinforce high performance?

506. Is this a Requirement?

507. Is staff trained on the software technologies that are being used on the Movie And Video Production project?

508. What would be the next steps or what else should you do at this point?

509. Is the amount of effort justified by the anticipated value of forming a new process?

510. Is the process working, and people are not executing in compliance of the process?

511. What is quality planning ?

512. What is the return on investment?

513. How relevant is this attribute to this Movie And Video Production project or audit?

514. Do you keep back-up copies of any data?

515. What are the appropriate test methods to be used?

516. Does the plan conform to standards?

517. How does your organization make it easy for customers to seek assistance or complain?

518. What are your organizations key processes (product, service, business, and support)?

519. Who gets results of work?

2.25 Quality Metrics: Movie And Video Production

520. Has trace of defects been initiated?

521. What group is empowered to define quality requirements?

522. Were number of defects identified?

523. Can you correlate your quality metrics to profitability?

524. Where did complaints, returns and warranty claims come from?

525. Are documents on hand to provide explanations of privacy and confidentiality?

526. Is material complete (and does it meet the standards)?

527. Has it met internal or external standards?

528. Are interface issues coordinated?

529. Are there already quality metrics available that detect nonlinear embeddings and trends similar to the users perception?

530. What method of measurement do you use?

531. Does risk analysis documentation meet

standards?

532. What metrics do you measure?

533. Subjective quality component: customer satisfaction, how do you measure it?

534. What is the benchmark?

535. Is quality culture a competitive advantage?

536. What if the biggest risk to your business were the already stated people who do not complain?

537. What are you trying to accomplish?

538. Which are the right metrics to use?

539. Are quality metrics defined?

2.26 Process Improvement Plan: Movie And Video Production

540. Are you meeting the quality standards?

541. Are you making progress on the goals?

542. Have storage and access mechanisms and procedures been determined?

543. How do you manage quality?

544. What lessons have you learned so far?

545. What personnel are the champions for the initiative?

546. Does your process ensure quality?

547. Why do you want to achieve the goal?

548. Does explicit definition of the measures exist?

549. What personnel are the change agents for your initiative?

550. To elicit goal statements, do you ask a question such as, What do you want to achieve?

551. Are there forms and procedures to collect and record the data?

552. Where are you now?

553. Who should prepare the process improvement action plan?

554. Where do you want to be?

555. Are you making progress on the improvement framework?

556. What is the test-cycle concept?

557. Everyone agrees on what process improvement is, right?

558. Are you following the quality standards?

559. Has a process guide to collect the data been developed?

2.27 Responsibility Assignment Matrix: Movie And Video Production

560. Wbs elements contractually specified for reporting of status (lowest level only)?

561. What are the known stakeholder requirements?

562. Identify potential or actual budget-based and time-based schedule variances?

563. Are the bases and rates for allocating costs from each indirect pool consistently applied?

564. Are indirect costs accumulated for comparison with the corresponding budgets?

565. Does the Movie And Video Production project need to be analyzed further to uncover additional responsibilities?

566. Is the anticipated (firm and potential) business base Movie And Video Production projected in a rational, consistent manner?

567. How cost benefit analysis?

568. The already stated responsible for the establishment of budgets and assignment of resources for overhead performance?

569. The staff characteristics – is the group or the person capable to work together as a team?

570. What expertise is available in your department?

571. No rs: if a task has no one listed as responsible, who is getting the job done?

572. Are the wbs and organizational levels for application of the Movie And Video Production projected overhead costs identified?

573. Are all elements of indirect expense identified to overhead cost budgets of Movie And Video Production projections?

574. Are overhead costs budgets established on a basis consistent with anticipated direct business base?

575. Are detailed work packages planned as far in advance as practicable?

2.28 Roles and Responsibilities: Movie And Video Production

576. Was the expectation clearly communicated?

577. Attainable / achievable: the goal is attainable; can you actually accomplish the goal?

578. Are Movie And Video Production project team roles and responsibilities identified and documented?

579. What is working well?

580. Is feedback clearly communicated and non-judgmental?

581. Do the values and practices inherent in the culture of your organization foster or hinder the process?

582. Implementation of actions: Who are the responsible units?

583. What expectations were met?

584. What expectations were NOT met?

585. Are the quality assurance functions and related roles and responsibilities clearly defined?

586. Is there a training program in place for stakeholders covering expectations, roles and responsibilities and any addition knowledge others

need to be good stakeholders?

587. Accountabilities: what are the roles and responsibilities of individual team members?

588. What should you highlight for improvement?

589. Concern: where are you limited or have no authority, where you can not influence?

590. Are your policies supportive of a culture of quality data?

591. Authority: what areas/Movie And Video Production projects in your work do you have the authority to decide upon and act on the already stated decisions?

592. What should you do now to prepare yourself for a promotion, increased responsibilities or a different job?

593. What areas of supervision are challenging for you?

594. Who is responsible for implementation activities and where will the functions, roles and responsibilities be defined?

595. Key conclusions and recommendations: Are conclusions and recommendations relevant and acceptable?

2.29 Human Resource Management Plan: Movie And Video Production

596. Has a quality assurance plan been developed for the Movie And Video Production project?

597. Are vendor contract reports, reviews and visits conducted periodically?

598. Measurable - are the targets measurable?

599. Is your organization certified as a supplier, wholesaler, regular dealer, or manufacturer of corresponding products/supplies?

600. What were things that you did well, and could improve, and how?

601. What is this Movie And Video Production project aiming to achieve?

602. Does the schedule include Movie And Video Production project management time and change request analysis time?

603. Is there an approved case?

604. Is an industry recognized support tool(s) being used for Movie And Video Production project scheduling & tracking?

605. How do you determine what key skills and talents are needed to meet the objectives. Is your

organization primarily focused on a specific industry?

606. Is there an on-going process in place to monitor Movie And Video Production project risks?

607. Have adequate resources been provided by management to ensure Movie And Video Production project success?

608. Is Movie And Video Production project status reviewed with the steering and executive teams at appropriate intervals?

609. Is a payment system in place with proper reviews and approvals?

610. Is there an issues management plan in place?

611. Alignment to strategic goals & objectives?

2.30 Communications Management Plan: Movie And Video Production

612. Is the stakeholder role recognized by your organization?

613. Who will use or be affected by the result of a Movie And Video Production project?

614. Do you ask; can you recommend others for you to talk with about this initiative?

615. Why do you manage communications?

616. Who needs to know and how much?

617. Timing: when do the effects of the communication take place?

618. Who are the members of the governing body?

619. How were corresponding initiatives successful?

620. Will messages be directly related to the release strategy or phases of the Movie And Video Production project?

621. Who have you worked with in past, similar initiatives?

622. What approaches to you feel are the best ones to use?

623. Do you prepare stakeholder engagement plans?

624. Why manage stakeholders?

625. What is Movie And Video Production project communications management?

626. What help do you and your team need from the stakeholder?

627. Who is the stakeholder?

628. Who were proponents/opponents?

629. Which stakeholders can influence others?

2.31 Risk Management Plan: Movie And Video Production

630. How is risk monitoring performed?

631. Are people attending meetings and doing work?

632. Why might it be late?

633. Mitigation -how can you avoid the risk?

634. Are team members trained in the use of the tools?

635. Risk probability and impact: how will the probabilities and impacts of risk items be assessed?

636. Are there risks to human health or the environment that need to be controlled or mitigated?

637. What does a risk management program do?

638. Is the necessary data being captured and is it complete and accurate?

639. Is the customer willing to commit significant time to the requirements gathering process?

640. What is the cost to the Movie And Video Production project if it does occur?

641. Can you stabilize dynamic risk factors?

642. Are the software tools integrated with each other?

643. My Movie And Video Production project leader has suddenly left your organization, what do you do?

644. Do benefits and chances of success outweigh potential damage if success is not attained?

645. Is the customer willing to participate in reviews?

646. Are certain activities taking a long time to complete?

647. What are it-specific requirements?

648. Are the reports useful and easy to read?

2.32 Risk Register: Movie And Video Production

649. What is a Risk?

650. What should the audit role be in establishing a risk management process?

651. What should you do now?

652. What can be done about it?

653. Contingency actions - planned actions to reduce the immediate seriousness of the risk when it does occur. What should you do when?

654. Are there any knock-on effects/impact on any of the other areas?

655. User involvement: do you have the right users?

656. Severity Prediction?

657. What may happen or not go according to plan?

658. When will it happen?

659. Can the likelihood and impact of failing to achieve corresponding recommendations and action plans be assessed?

660. Risk categories: what are the main categories of risks that should be addressed on this Movie And

Video Production project?

661. How is a Community Risk Register created?

662. How could corresponding Risk affect the Movie And Video Production project in terms of cost and schedule?

663. How are risks graded?

664. Who needs to know about this?

665. How well are risks controlled?

666. What are the assumptions and current status that support the assessment of the risk?

2.33 Probability and Impact Assessment: Movie And Video Production

667. Does the software engineering team have the right mix of skills?

668. Will new information become available during the Movie And Video Production project?

669. How do risks change during a Movie And Video Production project life cycle?

670. What is the level of experience available with your organization?

671. Do the people have the right combinations of skills?

672. Are end-users enthusiastically committed to the Movie And Video Production project and the system/ product to be built?

673. Which of your Movie And Video Production projects should be selected when compared with other Movie And Video Production projects?

674. How carefully have the potential competitors been identified?

675. Is the customer technically sophisticated in the product area?

676. Do you use diagramming techniques to show cause and effect?

677. What are the tools and techniques used in managing the challenges faced?

678. How do you define a risk?

679. Does the software interface with new or unproven hardware or unproven vendor products?

680. What will be the impact or consequence if the risk occurs?

681. Are there alternative opinions/solutions/ processes you should explore?

682. What are the industrial relations prevailing in your organization?

683. Which role do you have in the Movie And Video Production project?

684. What are the current or emerging trends of culture?

2.34 Probability and Impact Matrix: Movie And Video Production

685. How much risk do others need to take?

686. Do you have specific methods that you use for each phase of the process?

687. What needs to be DONE?

688. Management -what contingency plans do you have if the risk becomes a reality?

689. Do you manage the process through use of metrics?

690. Are compilers and code generators available and suitable for the product to be built?

691. Do others match with the clients requirement?

692. How well is the risk understood?

693. Can the Movie And Video Production project proceed without assuming the risk?

694. What are the risks involved in appointing external agencies to manage the Movie And Video Production project?

695. Amount of reused software?

696. What would be the effect of slippage?

697. Does the customer understand the software process?

698. Several experts are offsite, and wish to be included. How can this be done?

699. Prioritized components/features?

700. How do you manage Movie And Video Production project Risk?

701. Which risks need to move on to Perform Quantitative Risk Analysis?

2.35 Risk Data Sheet: Movie And Video Production

702. What is the environment within which you operate (social trends, economic, community values, broad based participation, national directions etc.)?

703. Potential for recurrence?

704. What if client refuses?

705. What actions can be taken to eliminate or remove risk?

706. Who has a vested interest in how you perform as your organization (our stakeholders)?

707. What is the chance that it will happen?

708. What do you know?

709. What are the main opportunities available to you that you should grab while you can?

710. How do you handle product safely?

711. Has a sensitivity analysis been carried out?

712. How can hazards be reduced?

713. Risk of what?

714. Do effective diagnostic tests exist?

715. What are the main threats to your existence?

716. Type of risk identified?

717. What is the likelihood of it happening?

718. Is the data sufficiently specified in terms of the type of failure being analyzed, and its frequency or probability?

719. What do people affected think about the need for, and practicality of preventive measures?

720. Has the most cost-effective solution been chosen?

2.36 Procurement Management Plan: Movie And Video Production

721. Are target dates established for each milestone deliverable?

722. Has a Movie And Video Production project Communications Plan been developed?

723. Is the Movie And Video Production project schedule available for all Movie And Video Production project team members to review?

724. What were things that you did very well and want to do the same again on the next Movie And Video Production project?

725. Are key risk mitigation strategies added to the Movie And Video Production project schedule?

726. What types of contracts will be used?

727. Are procurement deliverables arriving on time and to specification?

728. Are software metrics formally captured, analyzed and used as a basis for other Movie And Video Production project estimates?

729. Are the Movie And Video Production project team members located locally to the users/ stakeholders?

730. Is there an on-going process in place to monitor Movie And Video Production project risks?

731. Does all Movie And Video Production project documentation reside in a common repository for easy access?

732. Has the Movie And Video Production project scope been baselined?

733. Similar Movie And Video Production projects?

734. Are tasks tracked by hours?

735. What is a Movie And Video Production project Management Plan?

2.37 Source Selection Criteria: Movie And Video Production

736. What is the effect of the debriefing schedule on potential protests?

737. Can you identify proposed teaming partners and/or subcontractors and consider the nature and extent of proposed involvement in satisfying the Movie And Video Production project requirements?

738. What instructions should be provided regarding oral presentations?

739. How do you ensure an integrated assessment of proposals?

740. What information is to be provided and when should it be provided?

741. When and what information can be considered with offerors regarding past performance?

742. Is experience evaluated?

743. What can not be disclosed?

744. In the technical/management area, what criteria do you use to determine the final evaluation ratings?

745. What information may not be provided?

746. How should the oral presentations be handled?

747. Has all proposal data been loaded?

748. How should comments received in response to a RFP be handled?

749. What should be considered?

750. What documentation should be used to support the selection decision?

751. Are evaluators ready to begin this task?

752. How can business terms and conditions be improved to yield more effective price competition?

753. In which phase of the acquisition process cycle does source qualifications reside?

754. What should clarifications include?

2.38 Stakeholder Management Plan: Movie And Video Production

755. What preventative action can be taken to reduce the likelihood a risk will be realised?

756. Does the resource management plan include a personnel development plan?

757. Are actuals compared against estimates to analyze and correct variances?

758. Were the budget estimates reasonable?

759. How will you engage this stakeholder and gain commitment?

760. Was trending evident between audits?

761. Who will perform the review(s)?

762. Are enough systems & user personnel assigned to the Movie And Video Production project?

763. Are there any potential occupational health and safety issues due to the proposed purchases?

764. Have all necessary approvals been obtained?

765. Why would you develop a Movie And Video Production project Execution Plan?

766. Who will the report(s) be delivered to?

767. Have external dependencies been captured in the schedule?

768. Are risk triggers captured?

769. Does the Movie And Video Production project have a Quality Culture?

2.39 Change Management Plan: Movie And Video Production

770. Is there an adequate supply of people for the new roles?

771. Have the business unit contacts been briefed by the Movie And Video Production project team?

772. Do you need a new organizational structure?

773. Different application of an existing process?

774. Who will be the change levers?

775. What are the training strategies?

776. Who will fund the training?

777. Has a training need analysis been carried out?

778. Is a training information sheet available?

779. Who might present the most resistance?

780. Is there a need for new relationships to be built?

781. What are the responsibilities assigned to each role?

782. Who will do the training?

783. How much change management is needed?

784. Have the business unit contacts been selected and notified?

785. What is the most positive interpretation it can receive?

786. How do you gain sponsors buy-in to the communication plan?

787. What prerequisite knowledge do corresponding groups need?

788. How frequently should you repeat the message?

3.0 Executing Process Group: Movie And Video Production

789. Is the schedule for the set products being met?

790. How can software assist in procuring goods and services?

791. What are the key components of the Movie And Video Production project communications plan?

792. How does a Movie And Video Production project life cycle differ from a product life cycle?

793. What are the critical steps involved with strategy mapping?

794. How well did the team follow the chosen processes?

795. If action is called for, what form should it take?

796. How does Movie And Video Production project management relate to other disciplines?

797. Based on your Movie And Video Production project communication management plan, what worked well?

798. How could you control progress of your Movie And Video Production project?

799. Who will be the main sponsor?

800. What is the critical path for this Movie And Video Production project and how long is it?

801. How well did the chosen processes produce the expected results?

802. How do you measure difficulty?

803. Were sponsors and decision makers available when needed outside regularly scheduled meetings?

804. Why do you need a good WBS to use Movie And Video Production project management software?

3.1 Team Member Status Report: Movie And Video Production

805. Will the staff do training or is that done by a third party?

806. When a teams productivity and success depend on collaboration and the efficient flow of information, what generally fails them?

807. Is there evidence that staff is taking a more professional approach toward management of your organizations Movie And Video Production projects?

808. Does the product, good, or service already exist within your organization?

809. Are your organizations Movie And Video Production projects more successful over time?

810. Do you have an Enterprise Movie And Video Production project Management Office (EPMO)?

811. How it is to be done?

812. What is to be done?

813. What specific interest groups do you have in place?

814. Are the attitudes of staff regarding Movie And Video Production project work improving?

815. How does this product, good, or service meet the needs of the Movie And Video Production project and your organization as a whole?

816. Does your organization have the means (staff, money, contract, etc.) to produce or to acquire the product, good, or service?

817. Does every department have to have a Movie And Video Production project Manager on staff?

818. Are the products of your organizations Movie And Video Production projects meeting customers objectives?

819. How can you make it practical?

820. How will resource planning be done?

821. The problem with Reward & Recognition Programs is that the truly deserving people all too often get left out. How can you make it practical?

822. Why is it to be done?

823. How much risk is involved?

3.2 Change Request: Movie And Video Production

824. Will new change requests be acknowledged in a timely manner?

825. Are there requirements attributes that are strongly related to the complexity and size?

826. How many times must the change be modified or presented to the change control board before it is approved?

827. Since there are no change requests in your Movie And Video Production project at this point, what must you have before you begin?

828. Will there be a change request form in use?

829. Is it feasible to use requirements attributes as predictors of reliability?

830. Should staff call into the helpdesk or go to the website?

831. How well do experienced software developers predict software change?

832. What kind of information about the change request needs to be captured?

833. For which areas does this operating procedure apply?

834. Who is responsible for the implementation and monitoring of all measures?

835. Are you implementing itil processes?

836. How fast will change requests be approved?

837. Change request coordination ?

838. Who is responsible to authorize changes?

839. How shall the implementation of changes be recorded?

840. What mechanism is used to appraise others of changes that are made?

841. What must be taken into consideration when introducing change control programs?

842. Which requirements attributes affect the risk to reliability the most?

3.3 Change Log: Movie And Video Production

843. How does this change affect scope?

844. Should a more thorough impact analysis be conducted?

845. Is the requested change request a result of changes in other Movie And Video Production project(s)?

846. Is the change request open, closed or pending?

847. Who initiated the change request?

848. When was the request submitted?

849. How does this relate to the standards developed for specific business processes?

850. When was the request approved?

851. Is the change request within Movie And Video Production project scope?

852. Is this a mandatory replacement?

853. Is the change backward compatible without limitations?

854. Does the suggested change request seem to represent a necessary enhancement to the product?

855. Do the described changes impact on the integrity or security of the system?

856. Is the submitted change a new change or a modification of a previously approved change?

857. Does the suggested change request represent a desired enhancement to the products functionality?

858. Will the Movie And Video Production project fail if the change request is not executed?

859. How does this change affect the timeline of the schedule?

860. Where do changes come from?

3.4 Decision Log: Movie And Video Production

861. How effective is maintaining the log at facilitating organizational learning?

862. Which variables make a critical difference?

863. Is everything working as expected?

864. What is the line where eDiscovery ends and document review begins?

865. Linked to original objective?

866. Who will be given a copy of this document and where will it be kept?

867. What was the rationale for the decision?

868. How do you define success?

869. At what point in time does loss become unacceptable?

870. With whom was the decision shared or considered?

871. What eDiscovery problem or issue did your organization set out to fix or make better?

872. What are the cost implications?

873. What makes you different or better than others companies selling the same thing?

874. What is the average size of your matters in an applicable measurement?

875. How do you know when you are achieving it?

876. How does provision of information, both in terms of content and presentation, influence acceptance of alternative strategies?

877. Meeting purpose; why does this team meet?

878. Decision-making process; how will the team make decisions?

879. Do strategies and tactics aimed at less than full control reduce the costs of management or simply shift the cost burden?

880. Who is the decisionmaker?

3.5 Quality Audit: Movie And Video Production

881. What happens if your organization fails its Quality Audit?

882. How does your organization know that its system for commercializing research outputs is appropriately effective and constructive?

883. How does your organization know that it is appropriately effective and constructive in preparing its staff for organizational aspirations?

884. Are all records associated with the reconditioning of a device maintained for a minimum of two years after the sale or disposal of the last device within a lot of merchandise?

885. How does your organization know that its system for managing intellectual property issues is appropriately effective, constructive and fair?

886. Is there a written corporate quality policy?

887. How do you indicate the extent to which your personnel would be expected to contribute to the work effort?

888. How does your organization know that its systems for assisting staff with career planning and employment placements are appropriately effective and constructive?

889. Is refuse and garbage adequately stored and disposed of with sufficient frequency to prevent contamination?

890. How does your organization know that its teaching activities (and staff learning) are effectively and constructively enhanced by its activities?

891. Are all employees including salespersons made aware that they must report all complaints received from any source for inclusion in the complaint handling system?

892. What review processes are in place for your organizations major activities?

893. Are complaint files maintained?

894. Is your organizations resource allocation system properly aligned with its collection of intentions?

895. Are people allowed to contribute ideas?

896. Is progress against the intentions measurable?

897. How does your organization know that its system for staff performance planning and review is appropriately effective and constructive?

898. How does your organization know that its policy management system is appropriately effective and constructive?

899. Are training programs documented?

900. Is your organizational structure established and each positions responsibility defined?

3.6 Team Directory: Movie And Video Production

901. How and in what format should information be presented?

902. Process decisions: are there any statutory or regulatory issues relevant to the timely execution of work?

903. Is construction on schedule?

904. What needs to be communicated?

905. When does information need to be distributed?

906. Process decisions: is work progressing on schedule and per contract requirements?

907. Who will talk to the customer?

908. Contract requirements complied with?

909. What are you going to deliver or accomplish?

910. Where should the information be distributed?

911. Timing: when do the effects of communication take place?

912. Process decisions: are contractors adequately prosecuting the work?

913. Does a Movie And Video Production project team directory list all resources assigned to the Movie And Video Production project?

914. Process decisions: which organizational elements and which individuals will be assigned management functions?

915. Where will the product be used and/or delivered or built when appropriate?

916. How will the team handle changes?

917. Who will report Movie And Video Production project status to all stakeholders?

918. How will you accomplish and manage the objectives?

3.7 Team Operating Agreement: Movie And Video Production

919. What is a Virtual Team?

920. Do team members need to frequently communicate as a full group to make timely decisions?

921. Are there influences outside the team that may affect performance, and if so, have you identified and addressed them?

922. What resources can be provided for the team in terms of equipment, space, time for training, protected time and space for meetings, and travel allowances?

923. What are the safety issues/risks that need to be addressed and/or that the team needs to consider?

924. Do team members reside in more than two countries?

925. Do you determine the meeting length and time of day?

926. Do you post meeting notes and the recording (if used) and notify participants?

927. Do you listen for voice tone and word choice to understand the meaning behind words?

928. Have you established procedures that team members can follow to work effectively together, such as a team operating agreement?

929. Must your team members rely on the expertise of other members to complete tasks?

930. Do you call or email participants to ensure understanding, follow-through and commitment to the meeting outcomes?

931. Do you use a parking lot for any items that are important and outside of the agenda?

932. Do you begin with a question to engage everyone?

933. Must your members collaborate successfully to complete Movie And Video Production projects?

934. To whom do you deliver your services?

935. How will you divide work equitably?

936. What individual strengths does each team member bring to the group?

937. What is teaming?

938. Did you delegate tasks such as taking meeting minutes, presenting a topic and soliciting input?

3.8 Team Performance Assessment: Movie And Video Production

939. To what degree do team members agree with the goals, relative importance, and the ways in which achievement will be measured?

940. To what degree does the teams purpose constitute a broader, deeper aspiration than just accomplishing short-term goals?

941. To what degree does the teams work approach provide opportunity for members to engage in fact-based problem solving?

942. How do you recognize and praise members for contributions?

943. Is there a particular method of data analysis that you would recommend as a means of demonstrating that method variance is not of great concern for a given dataset?

944. To what degree will team members, individually and collectively, commit time to help themselves and others learn and develop skills?

945. Do friends perform better than acquaintances?

946. Social categorization and intergroup behaviour: Does minimal intergroup discrimination make social identity more positive?

947. To what degree do team members feel that the purpose of the team is important, if not exciting?

948. To what degree is the team cognizant of small wins to be celebrated along the way?

949. To what degree can the team ensure that all members are individually and jointly accountable for the teams purpose, goals, approach, and work-products?

950. What makes opportunities more or less obvious?

951. If you have criticized someones work for method variance in your role as reviewer, what was the circumstance?

952. To what degree will the approach capitalize on and enhance the skills of all team members in a manner that takes into consideration other demands on members of the team?

953. Do you give group members authority to make at least some important decisions?

954. Can team performance be reliably measured in simulator and live exercises using the same assessment tool?

955. To what degree are the skill areas critical to team performance present?

956. How do you encourage members to learn from each other?

957. To what degree are staff involved as partners in

the improvement process?

958. How do you keep key people outside the group informed about its accomplishments?

3.9 Team Member Performance Assessment: Movie And Video Production

959. Are there any safeguards to prevent intentional or unintentional rating errors?

960. Does the rater (supervisor) have the authority or responsibility to tell an employee that the employees performance is unsatisfactory?

961. What are acceptable governance changes?

962. What is used as a basis for instructional decisions?

963. What happens if a team member receives a Rating of Unsatisfactory?

964. How do you currently use the time that is available?

965. How do you create a self-sustaining capacity for a collaborative culture?

966. Who is responsible?

967. What, if any, steps are available for employees who feel they have been unfairly or inaccurately rated?

968. Why were corresponding selected?

969. What are best practices in use for the performance measurement system?

970. Is it clear how goals will be accomplished?

971. Are any validation activities performed?

972. Does platform-specific assessment information contribute to training placement or tailoring of instruction (e.g. aptitude-treatment interaction)?

973. How will you identify your Team Leaders?

974. Are assessment validation activities performed?

975. Should a ratee get a copy of all the raters documents about the employees performance?

976. What makes them effective?

977. What changes do you need to make to align practices with beliefs?

978. What future plans (e.g., modifications) do you have for your program?

3.10 Issue Log: Movie And Video Production

979. Is there an important stakeholder who is actively opposed and will not receive messages?

980. Do you often overlook a key stakeholder or stakeholder group?

981. What date was the issue resolved?

982. What is the status of the issue?

983. How do you manage human resources?

984. What help do you and your team need from the stakeholders?

985. Is the issue log kept in a safe place?

986. Which stakeholders are thought leaders, influences, or early adopters?

987. What approaches do you use?

988. Persistence; will users learn a work around or will they be bothered every time?

989. In classifying stakeholders, which approach to do so are you using?

990. Can you think of other people who might have concerns or interests?

991. Are the Movie And Video Production project issues uniquely identified, including to which product they refer?

992. What does the stakeholder need from the team?

993. What is the stakeholders level of authority?

994. What is a Stakeholder?

995. Are there potential barriers between the team and the stakeholder?

4.0 Monitoring and Controlling Process Group: Movie And Video Production

996. Does the solution fit in with organizations technical architectural requirements?

997. How was the program set-up initiated?

998. Is the verbiage used appropriate and understandable?

999. Propriety: who needs to be involved in the evaluation to be ethical?

1000. Who needs to be involved in the planning?

1001. Have operating capacities been created and/or reinforced in partners?

1002. How is agile portfolio management done?

1003. What resources (both financial and non-financial) are available/needed?

1004. Did the Movie And Video Production project team have enough people to execute the Movie And Video Production project plan?

1005. Were decisions made in a timely manner?

1006. In what way has the program come up with innovative measures for problem-solving?

1007. Were escalated issues resolved promptly?

1008. What input will you be required to provide the Movie And Video Production project team?

1009. Where is the Risk in the Movie And Video Production project?

1010. How are you doing?

1011. What business situation is being addressed?

4.1 Project Performance Report: Movie And Video Production

1012. To what degree are the tasks requirements reflected in the flow and storage of information?

1013. How will procurement be coordinated with other Movie And Video Production project aspects, such as scheduling and performance reporting?

1014. To what degree is there centralized control of information sharing?

1015. To what degree do the relationships of the informal organization motivate taskrelevant behavior and facilitate task completion?

1016. To what degree do team members articulate the teams work approach?

1017. What degree are the relative importance and priority of the goals clear to all team members?

1018. To what degree can team members meet frequently enough to accomplish the teams ends?

1019. To what degree are fresh input and perspectives systematically caught and added (for example, through information and analysis, new members, and senior sponsors)?

1020. How is the data used?

1021. To what degree are the structures of the formal organization consistent with the behaviors in the informal organization?

1022. To what degree are the goals realistic?

1023. To what degree does the team possess adequate membership to achieve its ends?

1024. To what degree does the information network provide individuals with the information they require?

1025. To what degree does the formal organization make use of individual resources and meet individual needs?

1026. To what degree are the members clear on what they are individually responsible for and what they are jointly responsible for?

1027. To what degree do members articulate the goals beyond the team membership?

4.2 Variance Analysis: Movie And Video Production

1028. Is budgeted cost for work performed calculated in a manner consistent with the way work is planned?

1029. There are detailed schedules which support control account and work package start and completion dates/events?

1030. Did your organization lose existing customers and/or gain new customers?

1031. Are records maintained to show how undistributed budgets are controlled?

1032. Budgeted cost for work performed?

1033. Are all budgets assigned to control accounts?

1034. Are records maintained to show how management reserves are used?

1035. Other relevant issues of Variance Analysis -selling price or gross margin?

1036. Are indirect costs charged to the appropriate indirect pools and incurring organization?

1037. Are there changes in the overhead pool and/or organization structures?

1038. Does the contractor use objective results,

design reviews and tests to trace schedule performance?

1039. How does your organization measure performance?

1040. How do you identify and isolate causes of favorable and unfavorable cost and schedule variances?

1041. How does your organization allocate the cost of shared expenses and services?

1042. What does an unfavorable overhead volume variance mean?

1043. How are material, labor, and overhead variances calculated and recorded?

4.3 Earned Value Status: Movie And Video Production

1044. Verification is a process of ensuring that the developed system satisfies the stakeholders agreements and specifications; Are you building the product right? What do you verify?

1045. Earned value can be used in almost any Movie And Video Production project situation and in almost any Movie And Video Production project environment. it may be used on large Movie And Video Production projects, medium sized Movie And Video Production projects, tiny Movie And Video Production projects (in cut-down form), complex and simple Movie And Video Production projects and in any market sector. some people, of course, know all about earned value, they have used it for years - but perhaps not as effectively as they could have?

1046. When is it going to finish?

1047. What is the unit of forecast value?

1048. If earned value management (EVM) is so good in determining the true status of a Movie And Video Production project and Movie And Video Production project its completion, why is it that hardly any one uses it in information systems related Movie And Video Production projects?

1049. Where is evidence-based earned value in your organization reported?

1050. How much is it going to cost by the finish?

1051. Where are your problem areas?

1052. Are you hitting your Movie And Video Production projects targets?

1053. How does this compare with other Movie And Video Production projects?

1054. Validation is a process of ensuring that the developed system will actually achieve the stakeholders desired outcomes; Are you building the right product? What do you validate?

4.4 Risk Audit: Movie And Video Production

1055. Do your financial policies and procedures ensure that each step in financial handling (receipt, recording, banking, reporting) is not completed by one person?

1056. What are the benefits of a Enterprise wide approach to Risk Management?

1057. How do you govern assets?

1058. Does your organization meet the terms of any contracts with which it is involved?

1059. Estimated size of product in number of programs, files, transactions?

1060. Are enough people available?

1061. Does your organization have a register of insurance policies detailing all current insurance policies?

1062. Do you have proper induction processes for all new paid staff and volunteers who have a specific role and responsibility?

1063. What limitations do auditors face in effectively applying risk-assessment results to the risk of material misstatement measures?

1064. Do requirements demand the use of new analysis, design, or testing methods?

1065. Do requirements put excessive performance constraints on the product?

1066. Is your organization able to present documentary evidence in support of compliance?

1067. Do you have position descriptions for all office bearers/staff?

1068. Improving fraud detection: do auditors react to abnormal inconsistencies between financial and non-financial measures?

1069. Are auditors able to effectively apply more soft evidence found in the risk-assessment process with the results of more tangible audit evidence found through more substantive testing?

1070. Do you record and file all audits?

1071. Are policies communicated to all affected?

1072. Does your organization have or has considered the need for insurance covers: public liability, professional indemnity and directors and officers liability?

4.5 Contractor Status Report: Movie And Video Production

1073. Who can list a Movie And Video Production project as organization experience, your organization or a previous employee of your organization?

1074. How long have you been using the services?

1075. What are the minimum and optimal bandwidth requirements for the proposed solution?

1076. Describe how often regular updates are made to the proposed solution. Are corresponding regular updates included in the standard maintenance plan?

1077. What was the final actual cost?

1078. What was the actual budget or estimated cost for your organizations services?

1079. Are there contractual transfer concerns?

1080. What was the budget or estimated cost for your organizations services?

1081. What process manages the contracts?

1082. What was the overall budget or estimated cost?

1083. How does the proposed individual meet each requirement?

1084. If applicable; describe your standard schedule for new software version releases. Are new software version releases included in the standard maintenance plan?

1085. What is the average response time for answering a support call?

1086. How is risk transferred?

4.6 Formal Acceptance: Movie And Video Production

1087. Did the Movie And Video Production project achieve its MOV?

1088. Have all comments been addressed?

1089. Who supplies data?

1090. Was the Movie And Video Production project work done on time, within budget, and according to specification?

1091. Does it do what client said it would?

1092. Was the Movie And Video Production project goal achieved?

1093. What are the requirements against which to test, Who will execute?

1094. What was done right?

1095. What features, practices, and processes proved to be strengths or weaknesses?

1096. Do you buy pre-configured systems or build your own configuration?

1097. Does it do what Movie And Video Production project team said it would?

1098. How does your team plan to obtain formal acceptance on your Movie And Video Production project?

1099. Was the client satisfied with the Movie And Video Production project results?

1100. Did the Movie And Video Production project manager and team act in a professional and ethical manner?

1101. What lessons were learned about your Movie And Video Production project management methodology?

1102. What function(s) does it fill or meet?

1103. Do you buy-in installation services?

1104. Was the Movie And Video Production project managed well?

1105. General estimate of the costs and times to complete the Movie And Video Production project?

1106. How well did the team follow the methodology?

5.0 Closing Process Group: Movie And Video Production

1107. Were the outcomes different from the already stated planned?

1108. If a risk event occurs, what will you do?

1109. What level of risk does the proposed budget represent to the Movie And Video Production project?

1110. What could have been improved?

1111. What were things that you did very well and want to do the same again on the next Movie And Video Production project?

1112. What is the Movie And Video Production project name and date of completion?

1113. What were things that you need to improve?

1114. Just how important is your work to the overall success of the Movie And Video Production project?

1115. Was the schedule met?

1116. What areas were overlooked on this Movie And Video Production project?

1117. What do you need to do?

1118. Was the user/client satisfied with the end

product?

1119. What can you do better next time, and what specific actions can you take to improve?

1120. What is the risk of failure to your organization?

5.1 Procurement Audit: Movie And Video Production

1121. Do your organizations policies promote and/or safeguard fair competition?

1122. Was timely and equal access to contract documents and information provided to all candidates?

1123. Were technical requirements set strict enough to guarantee the desired performance without being unnecessarily tight to exclude favourable bids that do not comply with all requirements?

1124. Are open purchase orders with a fixed monetary limitation used for local purchases of small dollar value?

1125. Are lease-purchase agreements drawn and processed in accordance with law and regulation?

1126. Were products/services not received within the prescribed time limit?

1127. Which are the main risks and controls of each phase?

1128. Are the users needs clearly and invariably defined and has the expected outcome or mission been clearly identified and communicated in measurable terms?

1129. Were results of the award procedures published?

1130. Are criteria and sub-criteria set suitable to identify the tender that offers best value for money?

1131. How do you confirm whether the contracted organization supplied the goods or executed the work as per the quality, quantity and price indicated in the contract agreement/ supply order?

1132. Where funding is being arranged by borrowings, do corresponding have the necessary approval and legal authority?

1133. Is funding made available for payments under the contract at the appropriate time and in accordance with the relevant national/public financial procedures?

1134. Has it been determined which shared services the procurement function/unit should be part of?

1135. Is there no evidence of favouritism towards a particular contractor during the evaluation and negotiation processes?

1136. In case of time and material and labour hour contracts, does surveillance give an adequate and reasonable assurance that the contractor is using efficient methods and effective cost controls?

1137. Are there complementary rules to be used and are they applied?

1138. Are tenders who do not comply with the

requirements specified in the request for tenders rejected?

1139. Was the estimation of contract value in accordance with the criteria fixed in the Directive?

1140. Are unusual uses of organization funds investigated?

5.2 Contract Close-Out: Movie And Video Production

1141. Are the signers the authorized officials?

1142. How does it work?

1143. How is the contracting office notified of the automatic contract close-out?

1144. Was the contract sufficiently clear so as not to result in numerous disputes and misunderstandings?

1145. Change in attitude or behavior?

1146. Have all contracts been completed?

1147. Have all acceptance criteria been met prior to final payment to contractors?

1148. Was the contract type appropriate?

1149. Was the contract complete without requiring numerous changes and revisions?

1150. Parties: Authorized?

1151. How/when used ?

1152. Has each contract been audited to verify acceptance and delivery?

1153. Parties: who is involved?

1154. Change in knowledge?

1155. What is capture management?

1156. Have all contracts been closed?

1157. What happens to the recipient of services?

1158. Have all contract records been included in the Movie And Video Production project archives?

1159. Change in circumstances?

5.3 Project or Phase Close-Out: Movie And Video Production

1160. What hierarchical authority does the stakeholder have in your organization?

1161. What benefits or impacts does the stakeholder group expect to obtain as a result of the Movie And Video Production project?

1162. Who controlled key decisions that were made?

1163. Who exerted influence that has positively affected or negatively impacted the Movie And Video Production project?

1164. What were the goals and objectives of the communications strategy for the Movie And Video Production project?

1165. Were cost budgets met?

1166. What was the preferred delivery mechanism?

1167. Planned completion date?

1168. What advantages do the an individual interview have over a group meeting, and vice-versa?

1169. If you were the Movie And Video Production project sponsor, how would you determine which Movie And Video Production project team(s) and/or individuals deserve recognition?

1170. Have business partners been involved extensively, and what data was required for them?

1171. Which changes might a stakeholder be required to make as a result of the Movie And Video Production project?

1172. Is there a clear cause and effect between the activity and the lesson learned?

1173. What is in it for you?

1174. What could be done to improve the process?

1175. Did the delivered product meet the specified requirements and goals of the Movie And Video Production project?

1176. How often did each stakeholder need an update?

5.4 Lessons Learned: Movie And Video Production

1177. Are corrective actions needed?

1178. What are the internal fiscal constraints?

1179. Were any strategies or activities unsuccessful?

1180. What regulatory regime controlled how your organization head and program manager directed your organization and Movie And Video Production project?

1181. How did the estimated Movie And Video Production project Budget compare with the total actual expenditures?

1182. What are the needs of the individuals?

1183. What are the funding priorities for intelligence?

1184. What is the impact of tax policy on the case?

1185. Were the aims and objectives achieved?

1186. What rewards do the individuals seek?

1187. Will the information remain current?

1188. If you had to do this Movie And Video Production project again, what is the one thing that you would change (related to process, not to technical solutions)?

1189. What are the conceptual limits of the research?

1190. What specialization does the task require?

1191. What are the Benefits of Measurements?

1192. How effective was each Movie And Video Production project Team member in fulfilling his/her role?

1193. What worked well/did not work well?

1194. Does the lesson educate others to improve performance?

1195. What was helpful to know when planning the deployment?

Index

Printed in Great Britain
by Amazon

27108596R00178